The Morality of Politics

The Morality of Politics

States, Honour and War

Ulf Hedetoft

ANTHEM PRESS

Anthem Press
An imprint of Wimbledon Publishing Company
www.anthempress.com

This edition first published in UK and USA 2025
by ANTHEM PRESS
75–76 Blackfriars Road, London SE1 8HA, UK
or PO Box 9779, London SW19 7ZG, UK
and
244 Madison Ave #116, New York, NY 10016, USA

Copyright © 2025 Ulf Hedetoft

The author asserts the moral right to be identified as the author of this work.

All rights reserved. Without limiting the rights under copyright reserved above, no part of this publication may be reproduced, stored or introduced into a retrieval system, or transmitted, in any form or by any means (electronic, mechanical, photocopying, recording or otherwise), without the prior written permission of both the copyright owner and the above publisher of this book.

British Library Cataloguing-in-Publication Data
A catalogue record for this book is available from the British Library.

Library of Congress Cataloging-in-Publication Data: 2025932223
A catalog record for this book has been requested.

Cover credit: Public Domain/ Wikipedia.com

ISBN-13: 978-1-83999-294-0
ISBN-10: 1-83999-294-8

This title is also available as an e-book.

CONTENTS

Introduction		1
1	Political Morality: A Critique of State-Citizen Relations	5
2	The Honour and Prestige of States	21
3	War, Peace and Morality: 10 Theses on the Cost of Freedom – and a Case Study of the War in Ukraine	51
Epilogue		75
References		77

INTRODUCTION

This book deals with the morality, honour, prestige and self-conception of states, all of which goes well beyond the narrow, rationalist defence of national interests, which dominates most International Relations (IR) studies. The honour of states – which is most clearly seen in situations of war – rests on the idealised conception of 'all of us', which includes all citizens, all classes and all generations, set against their opposite numbers outside of 'our' immediate sphere of domination. This state-based image of itself and its existential teleology constitutes its very essence, notwithstanding that it is often seen as a deviation ('exception') from the normal state of affairs, where the state is 'just' there to serve and support the economy and its principal actors.[1]

The volume, which is particularly topical given the current belligerent state of Europe and the global struggle for hegemony, pursues this line of thinking along three different but interconnected routes. The first chapter delves into the morality question itself, tackling the complex relationship between politics, law and morals and between states and citizens. The universe of moral judgements feeds off rigid distinctions between good and bad, I/we and the Other, liberty and restraint. Political actors support it, law legitimates it and citizens enact it.

The second chapter deals with the question of the honour and prestige of states, historically and conceptually. This is a question that has mostly been ignored, downplayed or misconceived by international relations theories, but which has now shown its renewed relevance and cries out for an explanation. The chapter argues not just that the honour of states matters, but also that whereas states in peacetime are mainly the servant of the economy and its leading representatives, in war and other extreme situations, the relationship

---

1 'Honour' is a core concept in this book. It refers to the positive, ideal self-image of states, their pride and self-appreciation, as well as their search for the respect, recognition and admiration of other states. In other words, it denotes the moral component of the reputation and self-respect of states, their mirror reflection in the imagined view of the others.

is turned upside down. This is when fighting for the national honour becomes the core issue, which sidelines all other political objectives and demonstrates the indispensable role of national morality.

The third chapter, therefore, tackles the question of war, peace and morality head-on. It starts by proposing 10 theses on the relationship between war and peace. The basic theorem is that war and peace are not contradictory but complementary: reasons for war are produced in times of peace. Both Kant's thesis on 'perpetual peace' and its modern corollary, that is, that democracies do not go to war against each other, are seen as fallacious. Further, war nullifies all democratic practices; internal peace must complement, and support, external conflict. Emergency becomes normality. The chapter ends by addressing the question of the background and rationale of the war in Ukraine, in the process critiquing the moral stance characterising the Western understanding of the situation.

Thus, all three chapters revolve around issues that relate to the interaction of war and democracy and the underlying morality that both legitimates and underpins the actions of politicians as well as citizens.

Throughout the book, the concept of 'monopolies of power' will be used to designate legitimate states. Max Weber referred to monopolies of violence or monopolies of force: 'Today [...] we have to say that a state is a human community that (successfully) claims the monopoly of the legitimate use of physical force within a given territory',[2] but as he admitted in the same article, 'force is certainly not the normal or the only means of the state – nobody says that – but force is a means specific to the state'. Doubtless violence and force can be and are often used to enforce the will of states, but, first, most states prefer for citizens to come to terms with their situation more pliantly, and, second, this is the basic rationale for political morality and its applications, which explains its popularity among political strata in developed democracies. Hence, 'monopolies of power' is a term which both encompasses the 'physical'/'violent' and the 'moral' sides of states' legitimate activities, both domestically within its own borders and internationally vis-à-vis competing sovereigns.

The book has as its primary focus the democratic states of the Occident: their identities, state-citizen relations, self-conception, sense of right and wrong, prestige-seeking, image of the Other, and the sensitive tipping points where 'peace' transforms into 'war' and states are willing to stake everything

---

2 Weber, 1921/2009, section 1.

for the sake of their honour. Reference will occasionally be made to more autocratic or 'dictatorial' types of states, but only as historical or conceptual mirror images of democracies and democratic practices. On the other hand, it will be demonstrated that the dividing line between democracy and fascism is more tenuous than normally imagined.[3]

---

3 A technical note on references: whenever an author appears with a surname followed by two different years, e.g. Weber, 1921/2009, the first year indicates when the text was first published, and the second the publication date of the article or book where the quotation originates.

Chapter 1

POLITICAL MORALITY: A CRITIQUE OF STATE-CITIZEN RELATIONS

Our whole philosophy is built on respect for the traditional moral values which are the cornerstones of a free society. All our policies are designed to encourage personal responsibility, personal initiative, self-respect and respect for others and their property.
(Margaret Thatcher)

Introduction: Morality and Current Debates

Today, everyone is a moralist. Citizens, as well as politicians, are adept at drawing lines between good and bad, between who they side with and who they regard as enemies. They know – or at least feel – that Putin is a despicable dictator and Zelenskyy, a fighter for freedom and democracy; that they live in a world where they – thank God – are allowed to elect their leaders, who subsequently do what they can to secure their life and happiness; that it is good to love animals and totally right that criminals are punished; that rooting for your country, in sport and war, is admirable, while criticising your nation is not; that lying, cheating, stealing and fornicating are sins, while leading a modest and ascetic life is virtuous; that you should not envy the rich and powerful, but rather be thankful for what they contribute to our welfare, growth and national unity; that bringing up children, working hard and paying your taxes should be your own contribution to the same project and so on.

All this seems so self-evident to citizens that they rarely reflect on the nature of their moral being, nor on why they themselves frequently overstep the line and commit breaches against the moral code. When they do so, they admittedly often do it with a guilty conscience, but this does not keep them from holding their fellow citizens on a tight moral leash and exposing their hypocrisy. The same applies to public debates, which use moral judgements liberally but hardly ever examine their rationale. Moralism, in other words, is there to be accepted and applied as a normative guideline for evaluation, action and behaviour, but not to be investigated and exposed for what it is.

This is even truer in respect of the most recent version of moral visions – that of the 'hyper' moralism of 'woke' communities.

Hence, there are good reasons to subject the morality of modern societies to deeper scrutiny than those at best offered by moral philosophy.[1]

What Is *Morality*?

The point of departure and the first thesis of this chapter is that an intimate but complicated connection exists between *morality* and *law*.[2] Laws set down the (shifting) political guidelines for what is allowed and what is not; this is 'the rule of law'. But laws are external to individuals, they assume the character of force and compulsion; laws must be obeyed as dictates. Morality, on the other hand, is the subjectivised version of law, the personalised interpretation of right and wrong, which transforms the 'must-do' of legal restrictions into the 'ought-to' of moral attitudes. Morality is law interiorised; 'law' transforms into 'justice', 'legitimacy', 'publicly condoned behaviour', or 'ethical standards'.

It is obvious that this opens the field for a multitude of moralistic versions of this, that and the other – including some that contradict the preferences of the state's legal position – and that standing firm on one's personal moral viewpoint may well run counter to the public morality of tolerance which ultimately characterises the ideal citizens.[3] Morality develops into a conscience

---

1 For an overview of moral theories in the philosophical domain, see *The Stanford Encyclopedia of Philosophy*, 2022. A particularly relevant feature of the philosophical debate about political morality relates to the question of immoral actions taken by political actors, the so-called 'dirty hands' debate, which was started by Michael Walzer in the 1970s. It hovers between the requirement on politicians to maintain ethical standards in all cases and the need in 'supreme emergency' to resort to actions that would normally be seen as immoral, inhumane, or what have you (the reckless bombing of entire cities, the dropping of nuclear bombs, etc.). For more on the subject, see e.g. Walzer, 1977; The Stanford Encyclopedia of Philosophy, 2023. In a general sense, the debate reflects the political dichotomy between cynicism (some call it realism) and morality.
2 The debate about the relation between law and morality is in itself nothing new: 'Law is essentially a set of rules and principles created and enforced by the state whereas morals are a set of beliefs, values and principles and behaviour [*sic*] standards which are enforced and created by society. Legal and moral rules can be isolated with the former being created by the legislative institution of parliament; whereas the latter have evolved with and through society and are the standards which society in general accepts and promotes' (LawTeacher, 2021). See also the account of the 1959 Devlin-Hart controversy in Blackman, 2021.
3 See the section on morality and tolerance below.

arena all its own, partially emancipated from the legal sphere that generated it, allowing for independent emotional and normative judgements of right and wrong, good and bad, acceptable and despicable. Thus, laws can be followed and referred to as the ultimate reference of moral verdicts, but it is also possible that people may condemn laws for being immoral, unjust and running counter to democratic legitimacy, respectively, to personal or collective interpretations of right and wrong.

The universe of moral judgements is rigidly dichotomous. It feeds off normative distinctions between good and bad, I/we and the Other, freedom and restraint. It is impervious to well-founded arguments; instead, it revels in emotive reactions and biased evaluations. Sympathy and disgust beat levelheaded thinking – either you are for or against, and the world of politics and law constantly intimates when you are on the right side. Outrage, scapegoating and righteous anger are the hallmarks of the moral citizen. Let's take a closer look at the origins of morality.

Morality, Law and Politics

Based on their legitimate power, democratic states subject citizens to *the law*, which has been designed by elected politicians and codified by governments. This is not surprising; in the words of Max Weber, '[s]ince the French Revolution, the modern lawyer and modern democracy absolutely belong together' (Weber, 1921/2009, section 51). States use their power to invest the rule of law with validity. In this way, they compel their citizens to acknowledge and respect their free (but mutually contradictory) interests. States in turn evaluate the actions of their citizens according to whether or not they conform to the legal requirements, and they validate their judgement by forcefully restoring breaches of the law (fines, sanctions, imprisonment). Thus, the actions of citizens become submerged within the legal framework. The end result is that citizens not just obey the dictates of laws, but also acknowledge their injunctions as an ethical yardstick, which they apply to themselves as well as others. They come to support 'law and order'.

Kant gave this relationship between morality and law his unconditional backing in *The Metaphysics of Morals*,[4] as well expressed by Paul Formosa:

> Freedom is not, for Kant, a complete lack of external hindrance, but the presence of the right sort of hindrance – namely, the legally enforced rule of right. [...] It is not the liberal right to pursue one's own private

---

4 Kant, 1797/1996.

conception of the good, but the public enactment of freedom in accordance with universal law (i.e. public autonomy), that is the founding value of Kantian justice. (Formosa, 2008, 160)

However, when states protect free private individuals – their persons and their property – by setting limits for them, this is not due to some *universal* law rooted in the ontology of human nature but to *social* laws, which the persons managing the affairs of the state, that is, the politicians, have seen fit to impose on them – interpreted by Kant as the rule of *right*.[5] Democratic states have, as their first and foremost task, to maintain societies in which the increase of private property *excludes* the majority of people from enjoying the benefits of societal wealth.[6] By projecting their power in such a way that no one with impunity can abuse persons or their property, states ensure, in the name of 'liberty and equality', that the differences existing in the economic sphere (as well as the contradictions they entail) run a course whose result is predetermined. The fact that the *same* legal treatment of social parties equipped with very *different* means is the best guarantee that social and economic *in*equality remains and grows is something that ardent supporters of egalitarianism refuse to recognise. For them, equality does not reveal a relationship of power; instead, it is seen as a normative ideal against which they measure and judge social differences.

The practice that matches this ideal is not, as such fantasies like to imagine, a *violation* of the rule of law but *the factual state* of the law. By comparing the actions of private persons with the contents of laws, states achieve their purported goal, that is, that the freedom of one person finds its limits at the next person's property. In this way, legal judgements are significantly different from those of science. Whereas scientific judgements constitute the theory of a given object, the explanation of it, which as thoughts and concepts maintains what it *is*, the judgements of the legal profession have nothing to do with explaining the actions that constitute their subject matter. What law *is* does not concern lawyers, for they know that the law *exists* as the result, not of scientific efforts but the *law-making processes* of the state. And they have only one

---

5 *The Metaphysics of Morals* subdivides into the Doctrine of Rights and the Doctrine of Virtues.
6 I refer to all types of persons who are excluded from the possession of landed or corporate property, and hence need to sell their labour power to the highest bidder. They are remunerated not with the value of their labour, that is, what they actually contribute to the production process, but only to the extent that satisfies the social need to secure the continued existence of their labour power. The state oversees that the property owners' desire to accumulate wealth does not endanger the very survival and accessibility of the workers, and hence constrains the freedom of *both* parties.

purpose, namely to examine the actions of citizens with a view to deciding if they contradict or conform with the current state of the law.

On the face of it, the consequent limitations and the unpleasant after-effects for citizens should lead most individuals not to condone the legal system and the *raison d'état* of lawmakers, but appearances are deceiving. For due to the benefits that private individuals pursue as free actors in the competitive system, they *will* the laws, which at the same time present themselves to them as a limitation; so, together with their benefits, they are forced to accept simultaneous restrictions. This is the ultimate source of morality: citizens justify their subjection to the power that restrains them with the ideal of the same power, and supplement their enforced servitude with the *virtues* that Kant applauded in the second part of *The Metaphysics of Morals*. This means that not only do citizens subject themselves to and obey the law, but in addition they adopt a moral attitude that allows them to come to terms with their obedience.[7] They measure their actions with the ideal of righteousness, and whilst constantly violating their duties as citizens in the pursuit of their sought-after benefits, they often do so with a guilty conscience. Over time, they may well get used to the hoped-for advantages to such an extent that they tend to forget evaluating their actions as good or bad, but the judgement of others constantly reminds them of it, in the same way that they themselves function as a guilty conscience for others; this is the root of public hypocrisy.

Morality is thus anything but superfluous background noise in the democratic arena. It is the subjectification of the limitations that citizens accept because of their own hopes for success in the competitive race – the attitude needed to come to terms with the self-restraint required if they want to 'make it' in the world.

Hence, it is no wonder that critique of this kind has difficulties being accepted by citizens steeped in moralistic attitudes – and not just moralism as an ideal, theoretical construct. Everybody – be it the fashion model, the industrial worker, the member of parliament or the First Lady – insists on *practising* the ideals of altruism, modesty, compassion and neighbourly love; everybody contributes their due to the fight against cancer, to the climate battle or Christmas charities. They gather in voluntary associations, convinced that there, finally, they have the chance to find meaningful communality,

---

7 As already mentioned in the previous section, individuals and groups choose their own way of interpreting the legal-political framework that they are compelled to respect, often by opting for solutions that seemingly diverge from this framework in more or less obvious ways, and not infrequently in accordance with their political preferences. Hence, moral universes subdivide into 'conservative', 'liberal', 'progressive', 'left-wing', 'anti-authoritarian' etc.

solidarity and friendship. They compensate the compulsion to compete with others through associations based on their ideals, even in cases when their idealism requires further sacrifices.

Morality and Religion, Morality as Religion

From a moral perspective, religion is crucial. Karl Marx accurately called Christianity the religion that most precisely matches capitalism:

> Für eine Gesellschaft von Warenproducenten, deren allgemein gesellschaftliches Produktionsverhältnis darin besteht, sich zu ihren Produkten als Waren, also als Werten, zu verhalten und in dieser sachlichen Form ihre Privatarbeiten aufeinander zu beziehen als gleiche menschliche Arbeit, ist das Christentum mit seinem Kultus des abstrakten Menschen, namentlich in seiner bürgerlichen Entwicklung, dem Protestantismus, Deismus usw., die entsprechende Religionsform. (Marx, 1867/1977, 93)[8]

Christian individuals practice the image of God as the supreme, all-powerful judge of their ability to manage both their good and evil sides:

> God has also given us a free will to seek and love what is true, good, and beautiful. Sadly, because of the Fall, we also suffer the impact of Original Sin, which darkens our minds, weakens our wills, and inclines us to sin. [...] Within us, then, is both the powerful surge toward the good because we are made in the image of God, and the darker impulses toward evil because of the effects of Original Sin. (United States Conference of Catholic Bishops, 2023)

Consequently,

> [w]e cannot speak about life in Christ or the moral life without acknowledging the reality of sin, our own sinfulness, and our need for God's mercy. When the existence of sin is denied it can result in spiritual and psychological damage because it is ultimately a denial of the truth about ourselves (ibid.)

---

8 'For a society of commodity producers, whose general social relations of production consist in relating to their products as commodities, that is as values, and in this objective form to connect their private products to each other as manifestations of abstract human labour, Christianity with its cult of the abstract human being, specifically in its bourgeois development as Protestantism, deism etc., is the corresponding religious form' (my translation).

So, everybody is a sinner, confesses it remorsefully, while simultaneously assuming the role of judge of other people's actions. That said, it is important to notice the differences regarding 'spiritual submissiveness' among the disciples of Christ. Some teach and preach the mandated morality to others – this has developed into a regular profession; others invent their own interpretation, their hypocrisy regarding Christian values and yardsticks assuming amateurish features. The state on its part (and the state churches) discovered the useful aspects of religious faith long ago and makes it continuously functional in the form of christenings, confirmations, weddings, funerals, church choirs, occasions of mourning, memorial days and so on. For the same reason, some states levy church taxes.

People who do not see themselves as religious devotees and often actually scorn religion are not left by the wayside, however. Atheists regularly take part in the above-mentioned events, for morality has become a religion unto itself, which no longer needs overtly religious support. People of the cloth have, on the one hand, reduced religious devotion to the practice of moral edicts (Grau, 2017, 62); on the other, they have opened the road for other ways of moral belief and behaviour, even some that may trump religion: 'If people don't follow the same rules, they will start fighting each other. You see this all the time in war zones when different groups of people have different values and beliefs about their *religion or land ownership*, but if everyone followed the same moral code, there would be no conflict between them because they would be working together instead of fighting each other' (Enlightio, 2022; my emphasis). Religion can be divisive, but a common adherence to moral sentiments, common altruism and general tolerance saves the day. The tables have been turned; morality does not *need* religion as a justification – it has become a religion all by itself.

Moralised Materialism: Morality as Weapon

As suggested above, however, the world of morality is not just beer and skittles, a rosy sphere of common harmony and peaceful collaboration. Behind the ideal lurks a darker reality, where material interests are not completely suppressed but have undergone a transformation into something less benign. Envy, jealousy, *Schadenfreude* and so on are sentiments rooted in materialism, but they have been turned into their negation. The fact that other people may seem to do well (or at least better than yourself) activates moralism as the denigration and rejection of these others: they have acted immorally or even criminally in order to achieve the benefits and have even done so *at your expense*. They have stolen your job (immigrants), your loved one (the other guys) or your hoped-for advancement (colleagues); they have therefore come into possession of the material goods and pleasures that rightfully belong to you. Hence they become situated on the evil side of the (your) world and are stereotyped as enemies. Should they fail in their endeavours, it serves them well, and you may even help that result along either through personal machinations or political lobbying (throw immigrants out!). Here, the Ten Commandments are easily forgotten; morality has become a weapon in your personal armoury. Morality and materialism have fused.

Hence, moralised materialism is a force to be seriously reckoned with in the competitive relations of the modern world. It is responsible for stereotyping, racism, hatred and outrage, but also for celebrations of Self and idealisations of selfish purposes. It is the perverted result of the trade-off between the egoism of private persons and the utopian existence of the same persons as moral citizens of the state. And it is also the area where individualised moralities, which may diverge significantly from the legally rooted and publicly condoned morality of the state, have a field day.

However, states require a lot more than jealousy and self-righteousness from their citizens as moral beings. The next level of requirement is called tolerance.

Morality and Tolerance

Imagine this situation: two people have an argument about work. One thinks having a job is mainly a way to make money and thus fend for yourself (and possibly your family), while the other views a job as a subjective-psychological necessity without which you would lose your self-respect (and possibly your identity as well). The discussion develops into a physical showdown – both parties violently defending their points of view, while hurling abuse at the other guy. Finally, the police intervene, keeping the brawlers apart and admonishing them to respect each other's perspectives, though they clearly contradict each other and cannot be mediated. In other words, the police – the representative of legitimate force in this case – instruct them to *tolerate* each other's contradictory points of view, to keep their peace and leave the other's position as it is. Or, differently expressed, to hang on to their positions as a private matter and not let their differences become public, let alone settled.

Opinions, beliefs and viewpoints belong in the private sphere. Citizens should be content with the right to express them, as long as they recognise their relative nature, do not make claims to their objective truth, and – if they must – practice them in one way only, that is, by transforming them into a party programme or joining an already existing party, while participating in the political competition for power within the institutional set-up designed for such ambitions. Otherwise, they have to remain within the parameters of the citizens' private sphere. Everybody can express their views, cultivate any belief they like, on condition that they recognise the right of others to do likewise, also and especially when the views/beliefs grate against each other. 'Tolerance is an important concept that helps people to live together peacefully. [...] Tolerance also means that you don't put your opinions above those of others, even when you are sure that you are right' (Rawat, 2022). Tolerance is the 'willingness to accept behaviour and beliefs that are different from your own, although you might not agree with or approve of them' (Cambridge Dictionary, 2022). Thus, interests can be voiced without being recognised *as such*. Also here, however, you have to tread carefully, for

> tolerance is possible only if we reduce moralization on every point of difference. [...] Moralization is, therefore, a *barrier* to tolerance because perceived immorality defines the boundaries of what can be tolerated. Since people consider matters of morality as objective, absolute and beyond compromise, attaching strong moral significance to every point of disagreement and difference makes tolerance almost impossible. (Yogeeswaran et al., 2021)

In other words, tolerance as a *public moral value* has to trump the moral, material and substantial content attached to the individual points under debate, that is, those issues with which the contestants are (morally) concerned. In philosophical terms,

> we encounter the *paradox of moral tolerance* [...]. If both the reasons for objection and the reasons for acceptance are called 'moral,' the paradox arises that it seems to be morally right or even morally required to tolerate what is morally wrong. The solution of this paradox therefore requires a distinction between various kinds of 'moral' reasons, some of which must be reasons of a higher order that ground and limit toleration. (Stanford Encyclopedia of Philosophy, 2022)

The public morality of tolerance occupies that 'higher order', since standing firm on the 'lower' means that private moralities tend to clash. This is the secret behind the much-vaunted pluralism and diversity of opinions in democracies, institutionalised in and by the public media, and celebrated as a lofty value: freedom of speech – but only within the boundaries set by public morality, and on condition that you either refrain from putting your opinions into practice or only do so without harming other individuals. Your interests have to stay theoretical or at least conform to the edicts of private property.

This, in turn means that the conflict between private individuals and the state is continued as a struggle within each person: between the private and the public side of individuals, between material interests and morality. States are not content with their subjects simply subordinating themselves for extraneous reasons (force), but require them to make this a personal-moral effort.

Morality and Nationalism

The state, however, is not a generic power holder; it is not universal but always a particular national state, which engenders its own specific nationalism and a matching morality. Nation states claim the loyalty and subservience of *their* citizens, which means that the identity of these citizens is required to match that of their nation state. In the words of Ralph Miliband, '[f]rom the point of view of dominant classes, nothing could be so obviously advantageous as the assertion which forms of one of the basic themes of nationalism, namely that all citizens, whoever they may be, owe a supreme allegiance to the "national interest" which requires that men should be ready to subdue all other interests, particularly class interests, for the sake of a larger, more comprehensive concern which unites in a supreme allegiance rich and poor, the comfortable and the deprived, the givers of orders and their recipients' (Miliband, 1973, 186).

Citizens should be proud to be a *particular* kind of citizen. To hold a passport tying them to X-state. To think that they were lucky to have been born in that special place with such a unique blend of landscape, habits, traditions, politics, history, emotions, sports, intellect and arts. And to be ready to defend their country when required to do so. In other words, they should be prepared to make sacrifices for their nation, its identity and its honour, because that is the morally right thing to do: in ordinary daily life to show self-restraint, work hard and raise your kids to be good citizens; in sports, academe and business to excel and make the state proud; and in extreme situations of conflict or war to practice the total elimination of your individual needs and interests. For the same reason, it is fine to be suspicious of foreigners and immigrants, who don't belong but just live here for selfish, opportunistic reasons. Ardent nationalists view democracy and hence the value of tolerance as fenced in by national borders and immigration as a threat to 'our way of life'.

Hence, public morality comes in as many state-condoned forms as there are real and would-be nations in the world; the morality of 'the others' is routinely denounced as fake, as inauthentic or construed and definitely as inferior to 'ours'. In the words of Alexander Grau, '[w]as in der einen Kultur erlaubt ist, ist in der anderen verboten. Was die eine Kultur gutheisst, ist in der anderen eine Todsünde. Moral gibt es nur im Plural' (Grau, 2017, 21).[9] Nationalism thus short-circuits the laudable characteristic of tolerance. The dress codes, eating habits, celebratory customs, languages, opinions and religions of foreigners are at best exotic features of foreign lands, to be experienced and relished as tourists or celebrated by the multicultural intelligentsia[10] but otherwise not something the ordinary folk are supposed to tolerate as an integral part of 'our' pluralism.

Morality and War

At no time is moralism more in demand than in situations of war. The reasons should be obvious from what has already been said. Wars – which draw rigid lines between right and wrong, Us and the Other – require the absolute and total sacrifice of individual life, the willing surrender of one's existence to the state – notwithstanding that wars actually annihilate every inkling of tolerance. Here, obeying orders, doing one's duty and killing the enemy are the word of the day.

War makes the difference between democracy and fascism disappear; in war situations differences of opinion are not allowed, elections are suspended, the opposition made powerless, direct orders the name of the game, the economy totally subsumed under the state, disagreement treason. Here everything is done in the name of 'exceptions' (Schmitt, 1932/2007), with the aim to secure the survival of the state. War is, in other words, fascism in practice.

People only count as material for mobilisation and manoeuvre and as prerequisites for winning the war. On the other hand, they must be equipped with the right morality to support and endure their suffering and (hopefully) return to a state of peace and freedom when the war is over, unless, of course, they pay the highest price and end up as heroes.

---

9 'What in one culture is allowed, is prohibited in another. What one culture supports, is a deadly sin in another. Morality only exists in the plural'.

10 Multiculturalism cultivates cultural relativism and cosmopolitan tolerance, and treats the relationship between states as if they were private individuals. The idealism of tolerance internationally is mainly represented by the UN, which has named 16 November 'the International Day of Tolerance': 'Tolerance is much more than passively accepting the other. It brings obligations to act, and must be taught, nurtured and defended. Tolerance requires investment by States in people, and in the fulfilment of their full potential through education, inclusion and opportunities. [...] On the International Day of Tolerance, let us recognise the mounting threat posed by those who strive to divide, and let us pledge to forge a path defined by dialogue, social cohesion and mutual understanding' (United Nations, n.d.).

It is noticeable that hardly anyone ever refers to – let alone documents – the fact that the defence of this much-vaunted freedom actually *pays off* for the ordinary citizen. Making citizens believe in the necessity of things in which they can see no advantage can only be performed by referring to *higher* values. In this respect, war actually resembles democracy in its state of normalcy. But whereas democracy is celebrated by media, intellectuals and politicians and also finds support among ordinary people, wars are accompanied either by philosophical discussions on whether or not they meet the criteria for 'just war'[11] or by moral condemnation, even though they might well be necessary, for, as always, the enemy is the one to blame and 'we' fight the righteous cause – that of freedom and human rights. That fight requires its own particular morality.[12]

Two Recent Moral Modulations

We cannot leave the moral hemisphere without dealing with two phenomena where morality not just exists as the accompaniment to more fundamental social structures but have taken over as the allegedly most significant aspect of life: hypermoralism and populism. One is purely moralistic, the second is an anti-elitist variant of political leadership.

In hypermoralism, moral issues like sex roles, diversity, environment and greening, veganism, anti-colonialism and open borders take centre stage and for the same reason acquire an intensity, a significance and an assertiveness hardly ever seen before. The field develops its own 'identitarian' culture wars. Ascetic lifestyles are celebrated. And trivial details are raised to the level of life-determining fundamentals. '[...] if there are enough women cabinet members, and in sufficiently powerful positions; how female ministers attend to their small children, too little or too much; whether the president of the Republic should use a motorcycle when visiting his lover [...]. With exciting issues like these filling the public space, who will want to hear about the entirely predictable failure of international financial diplomacy to agree on meaningful regulation of offshore banking and the shadow banking system?' (Streeck, 2017, 188–189).

This is what the German intellectual Alexander Grau has dubbed hypermoralism (Grau, 2017): 'Der Gegenwurf zum freien Markt ist der enthaltsame, sittenstrenge Asket, der den Verlockungen der zivilisierten Welt

---

11 See e.g. Fisher, 2012; Walzer, 1977; Wikipedia, 2023.
12 Further on states, war and morality, see Chapter 3.

widersteht und die Gesellschaft zur Umkehr aufruft' (ibid., 26).[13] This 'moralische Wahrheit ist zeitlos'[14] and does not give a damn about historical or other explanations.[15] 'Woke' people supplement their enforced subordination under the strictures that accompany their status as citizens (freedom/duties) with an enthusiastic personal-moral subjectification of the puritan asceticism the strictures have given rise to. As a consequence, they condemn the past for not living up to the harsh, timeless demands of their moral community: 'Vergangene Epochen und ihre Menschenbilder sind daher nicht nur anders, sie sind verwerflich, also inhuman, rassistisch, sexistisch oder auch was immer' (51).[16] Hypermoralism is – without realising, of course – the 'intellektuelle Überbau zur wirtschaftlichen Globalisierung [...] in der sich die Menschheit endgültig zum zeitlos Guten emporschwingt – zum weltweiten Edelmenschentum' (55).[17]

At bottom, 'woke' moralists factually advocate for a pure, unadulterated capitalism, unfettered by limitations of race, gender, nationality or religion and populated solely by morally clean, ascetic and environmentally conscious citizens. Then, but only then, can they support 'society'. David Runciman has argued that 'democracy is civil war without the fighting' (2018, 14), which effectively means that democracy is a way to avoid 'civil war' by requesting 'moderation' and 'tolerance' from citizens whenever their interests are at stake. In this newest version, however, the fighting is back but is now conducted – harshly and with little forgiveness – over moralistic rather than economic, social or political issues among self-righteous citizens, insulated, like the elites, from the concerns of ordinary human beings.[18]

A less radical, more mainstream and extremely popular version of identitarian moralism primarily celebrates sexual diversity and multicultural lifestyles. This version is currently spearheaded by homosexuals and transpersons and finds its apogee in 'rainbow' organisations and events, which have

---

13 'As a contrast to the free market we find the abstemious, highly moralistic ascetic, who resists the temptations of the civilized world and calls out for society to change its ways' (this and the following translations from the German original are mine).
14 'Moral truth is timeless'.
15 On the critique of wokeism, cancel culture, etc., see also the level-headed analysis in Kovalik, 2021.
16 'Past epochs and their views of human beings are not just different, they are reprehensible, ie inhuman, racist, sexist, and what have you.'
17 'Intellectual superstructure of economic globalization [...] where humanity finally rises to the level of endless goodness – to that of the universal nobility of humanity'.
18 This must be understood correctly. Young 'woke' people are of course also 'ordinary human beings', but *as citizens* they have chosen to adopt an extreme puritanical moralism, which de facto drowns out their material interests as private individuals.

managed to attract the support of multiple organisations (state as well as private), citizenship groups and media. The underlying message is both simple and compelling: everybody should not just be allowed to have their own way of adapting to society, but this is a 'human right' and something to be proud of too. Behind the much-vaunted 'diversity' thus lurks a deafening uniformity, which everybody is expected to recognise and come to terms with: that of the labour market and the economic structures of society, including its property rights. Contrary to appearances, however, this morality is far from new. In its more mundane forms, it might be recognised as a core feature of religious and ethnic diversity, institutionalised and celebrated by democratic moralism. Hence, it is not at all surprising that most contemporary societies embrace the movement: as long as individuals fulfil their most basic duties (family, upbringing and work), *how* they come to terms with the same duties is their own personal business and worth public acclaim as well.

The second response to the perceived decline of 'normal' democracy is more expressly political, but no less moralistic. It is called populism – a moralistic reinterpretation of political nationalism (Hedetoft, 2020), which incidentally condemns hypermoralism as 'political correctness'. Populists stand firm on religion, family values and national sovereignty, raising national culture and identity to new levels of moral justification and ontological existence – in the process claiming to represent the people and its interests, while calling on divine intervention to clinch this holy alliance. This happens in Poland and Hungary, in different formats and in several other movements and countries too.

The two forms of moralism engage in their own peculiar form of interaction. For instance, the rainbow movement condemns the Orbán regime in Hungary for its intolerance towards sexual minorities in explicitly moral terms, to which the regime, no less moralistically, responds by referring to the Hungarian family tradition, which in turn is consecrated by religion and the support of the popular majority. The two forms of moralism defend each their own kind of worldview and are increasingly fighting out a struggle reminiscent of the Morality Plays of the Middle Ages.[19]

---

19 'Morality play, also called morality, an allegorical drama popular in Europe especially during the 15th and 16th centuries, in which the characters personify moral qualities (such as charity or vice) or abstractions (as death or youth) and in which moral lessons are taught. Together with the mystery play and the miracle play, the morality play is one of the three main types of vernacular drama produced during the Middle Ages' (Britannica, n.d.).

The Morale of Morality

Morality is not a sideshow but the guarantee that citizens support the ruling order and are fittingly enthusiastic, emotional, dismissive and properly scandalised. Moralism represents a disconnect between rational thinking and feelings and a bond between individuals, law and politics. In a rare bout of insight, the editors of Enlightio (2022) phrase this bond as follows: 'Morality is often used as a means to control people's behavior. Religious leaders, for example, use morality to convince people to follow their teachings. Politicians may use moral appeals to gain support for their policies. Advertisers may also use moral appeals to sell products'. They even acknowledge the link between morality and law, albeit in a roundabout kind of way, which confuses cause and effect: '[…] morality is an important part of the law because it helps determine what is considered harmful behavior'. However, these glimpses of insight are rare and only serve the overall purpose of celebrating all the positive and indispensable values connected with morality: it fosters 'social cohesion and harmony' and 'makes the world a better place'. In brief, it is 'the foundation of societies and civilizations'. In other words, those who use morality to control people allegedly abuse it and pervert its true purpose and teleology.

Not so, however. In fact, moralism ensures that democratic societies are equipped with individuals able to make a mature, responsible separation between good and evil, heroes and villains and between their own dual roles as competitive persons and citizens. It ensures the free and willing subordination of the people under the objectives of state and economy, whilst convincing the same people that their support is grounded in their *own* commonsensical emotions, deep-seated feelings of righteousness and intuitive distinctions between right and wrong. Where morality for citizens thus serves as way to assess and guide their lives, for the state it is a convenient instrument – with the exception of 'extreme' situations of emergency, when the state elites themselves discover morality and honourable goals as ends in themselves.

****

This chapter has dealt critically with the moral questions that arise in the interaction between states and citizens, both with respect to domestic affairs and in the international arena. States regularly appeal to the moral sentiments of their citizens, especially when they feel compelled to impose less pleasant restraints on them and require them to sacrifice income, leisure time or – in the last resort – their lives for the greater communal good. Democratic states on this count have an edge compared with power monopolies less firmly rooted in the popular will: they can – and do – routinely remind citizens that the incumbent politicians have been duly elected by the same citizens and hence do what they do with the backing and approval of the people. *Quod erat demonstrandum!* Politicians are practical philosophers when they appeal to the identity, national pride and honourable self-sacrifice of their subjects.

The next chapter will investigate, theoretically and historically, the same moral issues as they emerge and transubstantiate in the interaction between states on the international stage. It will demonstrate that power monopolies have moralities of their own and that not all their actions are determined by economic interests and instrumental *Realpolitik*.

Chapter 2

THE HONOUR AND PRESTIGE OF STATES

Has there ever been a great Commander destitute of the love of honour, or is such a character even conceivable?

(Carl von Clausewitz)

Introduction

In the relatively scant academic literature on the honour and prestige of states,[1] states are often treated as if they were human beings eager to defend their good name or vindicate their personal reputation. And while there are certainly affinities between personal repute and the prestige of states, I will argue that this line of thinking basically misses the central point when it comes to explaining what's really at stake when, for instance, states seek revenge to make up for their damaged reputation, bask in the admiration or jealousy of like-minded entities due to some economic or political success or do their utmost to occupy the top spot on international ranking lists (be it of welfare, democracy, happiness or what have you). States, unlike individuals, are power monopolies, but their monopoly of force only counts *as such* within their own areas of sovereignty. Whatever other influence they might wield is dependent on their success on the international scene, in their interaction with other power monopolies, which all strive to enhance their external reach and/or their international prestige. Whenever their striving for power is successful, they potentially add to their international standing, but when it is not,

---

1 Most contributions related to 'honour' have been produced by anthropologists and philosophers (e.g. Berger, 1983; Bowman, 2006; Peristiany & Pitt-Rivers, 2005; Welsh, 2008), but there are some within the field of politics and IR. See e.g. Aron, 1973; Ay, 2004; Kagan, 1997; Khong, 2019; Kim, 2004; Mansoor, 2015; Markey, 1999; Morgenthau, 1949 and 1979; O'Neill, 1999 and 2002; Thornton, 2017; Wood, 2014. 'Honour' and 'prestige' are related concepts, but not synonyms – see below.

they will do almost anything to restore their honour, sometimes even go to war.

In most cases, therefore, honour, power and interest are closely linked, but states occasionally pursue idealistic goals and defend their prestige for its own sake and with little regard for the ultimate consequences. In the words of Winston Churchill, when, in 1940, he decided to take on the imminent threat of German Nazism, he was guided by 'emotions which lead me to stake our all upon duty and honour' (Cannadine, 1990, 175). Donald Kagan was apparently right: 'For the last 2500 years, at least, states have conducted their affairs and often gone to war moved by considerations that would not pass the test of "vital national interests" [...] persisting in this course even when the danger has been evident and the cost high' (Kagan, 1997). States are used to having their way, and even when this does not pan out as planned, they are ready to 'stake [their] all' to vindicate their existence and show that at least when it comes to bravery, heroism and sacrifice, they are second to none. States have their own morality. They define for themselves what constitutes their pride and identity – which is helped along by the fact that, even when they lose, they rarely die (though many of their citizens might), and they always have, or imagine having, a chance to revenge themselves, regain their old position, repair their identity, repossess lost territories and finally end up on top again. This goes well beyond the narrow, rationalist defence of national interests. It rests on the ideal conception of 'our all', which includes all citizens, all classes and all generations, set against their opposite numbers outside of 'our' immediate sphere of domination. Let us, for a start, review a few examples where national honour means something in the international world of states.

National Honour Exemplified

Example 1. *National honour and economics*. Recently Crédit Suisse, a giant Swiss bank on the brink of bankruptcy, was taken over by another huge Swiss bank, UBS, with the financial help of the Swiss state. This was obviously an economic and financial calamity with great national and international repercussions, but it was also a scar on Swiss identity and a blemish to the national honour:

> The demise of one of Switzerland's oldest institutions has come as a shock to many of its citizens. Credit Suisse is 'part of Switzerland's identity,' said Hans Gersbach, a professor of macroeconomics at ETH university in Zurich. The bank 'has been instrumental in the development of modern Switzerland.'

Its collapse has also tainted Switzerland's reputation as a safe and stable global financial centre, particularly after the government effectively stripped shareholders of voting rights to get the deal done.

Swiss authorities also wiped out some bondholders ahead of shareholders, upending the traditional hierarchy of losses in a bank failure and dealing another blow to the country's reputation among investors.

> 'The repercussions for Switzerland are terrible,' said Bris of IMD. 'For a start, the reputation of Switzerland has been damaged forever'. (Ziady, 2023)

The 'forever' might be an exaggeration, however. The World Economic Forum, held every year in Davos, will do its bit to remedy the disaster: 'In terms of prestige, hosting the WEF is not just about navigating global dialogues. It showcases Switzerland's status as a hub for international business and politics, translating diplomatic gatherings into tangible economic benefits', as pointed out by Aude Ghespière in a contribution to *Leaders League* titled 'The WEF in Davos – A Platform Boosting Swiss Prestige and Economy' (Ghespière, 2024). The Crédit Suisse blemish is transitory, unlike the next example.

Example 2. *Brexit and British honour.* In an opinion piece titled 'Brexit has devastated Britain's international reputation – and respect for its democracy' (The Washington Post, 12 March 2019), Anne Applebaum wrote as follows on the international prestige of Britain:

> It's worth pausing to reflect on the damage already done by the Brexit debacle, and I don't mean the harm to the economy. Far worse is the damage done to Britain's reputation as a serious international player, a competent negotiator of treaties, a reliable ally, a voice for sense in the world – and a representative democracy. My Spanish and Italian acquaintances are not alone in their astonishment: All across Europe, people are reassessing their views of Britain, its politics and above all its politicians. (Applebaum, 2019)

Sentiments of this nature are no doubt shared by British citizens who do not agree with the exit of the UK from the EU. For the Brexiteers, on the other hand, the question of prestige and honour looks very different. For them, Britain was becoming dishonourably swallowed up in and by the 'European Empire',[2] and the 'honourable' thing to do was therefore to salvage British

---

2 In Boris Johnson's words, 'what we want is for Britain to be like many other countries in having free-trade access to the territory covered by the Single Market–but not to be

sovereignty, self-respect and identity by waving goodbye to Brussels. In this way, Brexit represents a clash of two competing visions of British honour rather than two ways ahead for the British economy. Recently, the Sunak government made amends and tried to re-enter the respectable international club by contributing massively to the Ukrainian war effort against the Russian invasion, a policy that the current Labour government has adopted and continued.

Example 3. *Honour and diplomacy.* Both Finland and Sweden have now been admitted to NATO, but whereas Finland achieved this goal relatively painlessly, Sweden's path proved to be a lot harder, lasting until March 2024. This was primarily due to resistance by Turkey, but Hungary also dragged its feet. The reason is illuminating:

> Though Hungary supports Sweden's NATO membership, Stockholm should stop spreading 'lies' about Budapest and its rule-of-law track record, a lawmaker from the Central European nation said on Tuesday.
>
> Csaba Hende, deputy speaker of the Hungarian parliament, told reporters in Stockholm that Sweden was disseminating 'lies' and that the country needed to treat Hungary with 'more respect,' according to Swedish broadcaster Sveriges Radio.
>
> 'It would be good if in the future, Swedish politicians, members of government, MPs and MEPs would avoid portraying Hungary in a false light,' Hende said, criticizing them for alluding to an absence of rule of law 'based on clearly untrue facts'. (Dönmez, 2023)

The geopolitics of NATO membership is often perceived as a matter of strategic alignment and shared defence interests. Yet, the case of Sweden's application reveals another and more intangible dimension: national honour. While Hungary does not seem to have any fundamental objections to Sweden's NATO membership from a security or strategic standpoint, its government felt that Sweden treated Hungary dishonourably and contributed towards a denigration of its international prestige. This obviously has no bearing whatsoever on the issue itself. Nevertheless, Hungary made a point of emphasising the significance of its damaged self-respect[3] and postponed its acceptance of

---

subject to the vast, growing and politically-driven empire of EU law' (Johnson, 2016). It must be added that Johnson did not use the term 'empire' scientifically/conceptually, but as a negative stereotype to brand the EU as an undemocratic opponent. Hence, he did not distinguish between, e.g.for example, 'empire' and 'federation'.

3 Hungary's damaged self-respect dates back to the humiliating experience of the Treaty of Trianon (1920), which significantly reduced both the Hungarian territory and the population of Hungary, and still gives rise to irredentist feelings and politics in Hungary.

Sweden on that account. This final acceptance only took place following a formal visit by the Swedish prime minister to Budapest in February 2024, which Hungary had demanded and which symbolically mitigated the country's injured self-respect.

Example 4. *The honour of France.* A prime example of a defence of the national honour is Charles de Gaulle, his resistance to the Nazi occupation of France and his protracted struggle for the sovereignty and 'splendour' of France:

> 'The flame of French resistance must not be extinguished and will not be extinguished.' [...] De Gaulle saw himself as nothing less than the keeper of the French flame, the custodian of the vaunted but now-embattled legacy of one of the great countries of the world. Traveling abroad for a meeting, de Gaulle was asked about his 'mission' and famously replied: 'I am not here on a mission, I am here to save the honour of France'. (Strachan, 2019)

There can be little doubt that de Gaulle and the Free French for several years fought an uphill battle that seemed destined to fail, but he persevered against the odds, became the president of France and thus 'kept the French flame' in the tradition of both Joan of Arc and Napoleon. It is fitting to call him an idealist of the French state and its identity, a person who was willing to 'stake (his) all' on his self-proclaimed role as a saviour of the French 'honour'. It is completely consistent with this idealism that he only supported The European Economic Community (EEC) as a 'Europe of States' and never embraced any federalist ambitions.

Example 5. *MAGA and American honour.* Donald Trump's first presidency was crucially about 'Making America Great *Again*' (my emphasis), that is, restoring the United States' (alleged) loss of world supremacy, politically, militarily and economically. In his farewell address (hardly noticed because of the attack on Congress on 6 January 2021),[4] Trump enumerated all the successes of his presidency in achieving his goals: rebuilding the military, boosting NASA and America's space enterprises, strengthening the economy, creating new jobs:

> Incomes soared, wages boomed, the American Dream was restored, and millions were lifted from poverty in just a few short years. It was a miracle. The stock market set one record after another, with 148 stock market highs during this short period of time, and boosted the

---

4 Trump, 2021.

retirements and pensions of hardworking citizens all across our nation. 401(k)s are at a level they've never been at before. We've never seen numbers like we've seen, and that's before the pandemic and after the pandemic.

We rebuilt the American manufacturing base, opened up thousands of new factories, and brought back the beautiful phrase: 'Made in the USA'. (Trump, 2021)

Externally, '[w]e revitalised our alliances and rallied the nations of the world to stand up to China like never before', which simultaneously lets the cat out of the bag: China is the chief competitor for world domination and the reason why the United States' global power is threatened.

However, the threat is not only directed against America's imperial supremacy, but also against its pride and self-image: 'We restored American strength at home and American leadership abroad. *The world respects us again.* Please don't lose that respect' (my emphasis). Whether or not this is a true representation of the state of affairs in early 2021, it reveals the close link between ambitions for power and ambitions for prestige; the United States wants not just to hang onto its 'leadership' of the world, but also wants to be recognised, respected and honoured for this achievement, both externally and at home:

Now, as I leave the White House, I have been reflecting on the dangers that threaten the priceless inheritance we all share. As the world's most powerful nation, America faces constant threats and challenges from abroad. But the greatest danger we face is a loss of confidence in ourselves, a loss of confidence in our national greatness. A nation is only as strong as its spirit. We are only as dynamic as our pride. We are only as vibrant as the faith that beats in the hearts of our people.

Example 6. *Honour, Russia and the West.* Russia – which incidentally is not mentioned in Trump's farewell announcement – also in this area represents a deviation from the normal order of things. Russia is less concerned with its overall international prestige and much more with holding on to its power, possessions and internal identity. Its relations with 'the West' have been ambiguous, ambivalent and contradictory for several centuries, while its most 'prestigious' success was the victory over Hitler's Germany, which on the one hand implied the loss of 20 million Russians and on the other pointed towards the Soviet loss of power, territories and self-respect in the Cold War. Julia Gurganus and Eugene Rumer in 2019 accurately articulated the Russian dilemma as follows:

Throughout Russian history since the time of Peter the Great, Russian elites, political thinkers, and cultural figures have questioned Russia's

European choice and relationship with Europe. In a more recent and very telling sign of that ambivalence, Foreign Minister Lavrov wrote in 2016 that, over the centuries, Russia has seen itself as part of Europe and the West, as better than the West, as different and unique from the West, and as representing a crucial link between the East and the West. The biggest obstacle that has kept Russia from having a closer and more stable relationship with Europe, according to Lavrov, has been Europe's inability or unwillingness to simply let Russia be Russia, and its insistence on having Moscow conform to European norms – something that no Russian leader or the people of Russia would ever accept. Moscow's claim to great power status has derived from its victories in the West, against Napoleon and Hitler. But Russia's biggest setbacks too have been delivered by the West – in the Crimean War and in the Cold War – and these setbacks remain the biggest drivers of Moscow's security and defense policy.

As was the case during the Cold War, Russian policy toward the West has long had an important ideological dimension. During the Soviet era, the ideological competition was between Soviet communism and democratic capitalism. After a relatively brief period when Russia attempted to join the West, Moscow has embraced an overtly anti-Western ideology. Communism has been replaced by a mix of nationalist, authoritarian, and state-capitalist ideas as an alternative to the West's notion of liberal democratic capitalism. The concept of Russia as a besieged fortress facing hostile Western designs and influences is a key tool the regime uses to mobilize the political support of Russian elites and ordinary citizens alike. (Gurganus & Rumer, 2019)

The main driver of Russian ambitions since the mid-1990s has therefore been to assert itself *against* 'the West' (the United States and Europe in particular), while attempting to recoup as much of the lost power as possible, rather than trying to win the recognition of the menacing Other. This does not mean that the question of national honour has been eliminated, but it has been transformed into a quest for domestic pride, solidarity and identity *as distinct from* international prestige. Whereas in the American case, the two – prestige and honour, international recognition and patriotic pride – interchangeably define each other, in the Russian case, they are kept separate. 'Our' honour depends on using Russian power resources and networks to bring the West to its knees, not to revel in its praise. Thucydides' trichotomy – fear, honour and interest – gets two different modulations in the two countries.

****

Countless other examples could be cited: Nazi Germany's revenge due to the humiliation of the First World War (WWI); North Korea's boisterously symbolic demonstrations of its nuclear potential; China's overt pride in its successful thousand-year history and its victory over the colonisers; Ukraine's military honour and international prestige being salvaged and increased on account of its persistent anti-Russian efforts. Modulations are as multiple as there are states. Now let us look more closely at the underlying patterns and causalities.

The Logic of Honour

The reputation of states stands at the top of the teleology of these partly idealistic entities.[5] Modern states basically have three goals in mind when carrying out their tasks: defending their interests (which includes their economies), often disguised as 'rights'; asserting their identities; and upholding their honour.[6] All three have material as well as ideational components, and all three are an amalgamation of external and internal (domestic) constituents. The triad bears echoes of the Thucydidean trichotomy of fear, honour and interest, which outlined the main drivers of state behaviour in the classical era.

Unlike the ancient Athenian perspective, where 'interest' was primarily tied to the state's capacity to wage war, modern interests are more multifaceted. In the case of ancient Athens, the economy served the single purpose of financing wars against the Spartans and their Peloponnesian League. Wealthy citizens and subjugated city-states paid 'tributes' to Athens, rising in its hierarchy of prestige. Overall, however, the line from interest to honour generally presents a development from (more) materialism to (more) idealism. The *interests* of states are concerned with developing financial, infrastructural and market-oriented relations to the benefit of domestic corporate entrepreneurs; *identities* mainly target the domestic unity of state and people and the social togetherness of classes, genders and generations; whilst *honour* implies the self-image, pride and prestige of the state itself. It is obvious that the three do not exist in isolation but constantly define each other and interact in a variety of ways. Interests may become defined by the history and self-image of states; identities may become threatened by domestic conflict or massive

---

5 Modern states are ideal constructions in the sense that they cater to the non-profitable but necessary needs of the economy and represent the communal glue between classes and national interests vis-à-vis other nations.
6 Despite these efforts, the long-drawn-out Peloponnesian War led to the defeat of Athens and the loss of its empire in 404 BC. (Thucydides, 1910 and 1998. See also Devereaux, 2019.)

immigration, while contributing to the development of new political interests or other ways of protecting (and projecting) the nation; and the defence of honour may become the principal interest when states are at war with competing entities and have little to show for themselves except the heroism of their dead and the morale of their surviving soldiers. Nevertheless, interests and power ambitions have a stronger and more obvious 'material' component (this is what so-called 'realists' tend to emphasise), while honour is dominated by 'nonmaterialist impulses' (Kagan, 1997). That the defence of a state's honour and prestige can lead to a successful defence of its interests – as was the case with Britain's opposition to Nazi Germany in the Second World War (WWII) or Ronald Reagan's reversal of Jimmy Carter's détente policy towards the Soviet Union – only goes to show that the political world cannot be captured by simplistic International Politics (IP) theorems.

Honour and prestige, though intimately linked, are concepts of a different nature. Honour covers the search for a proud self-image for the sake of which states are willing to 'stake (their) all'. Prestige (or reputation) refers to a state's relative standing in the international world of states, to the (real or imagined) view and evaluation of it by other states, and 'is valued both as an end and as a means [to obtain more power]' (Khong, 2019). And where honour (an absolute concept) can, in principle, be achieved in its dealings with any other international competitor (politically, militarily, in sports etc.), prestige (a relative notion) only counts in comparison with or among likeminded entities, most often democracies. Hence, Ukraine's honour is at stake in its conflict with Russia, but it can gather prestige among Western countries eager to assist it in the fight, with which it compares itself and which it hopes to join (the EU, NATO). Russia, conversely, has its honour in mind in its war against Ukraine and its conflict with NATO, but it cannot hope to increase its international prestige on that count, at least only as far as the 'Global South', North Korea and possibly China are concerned. This is where democracies and autocracies part ways. They can only achieve honour *against* each other and prestige *with* each other. This (modern) fact also implies that democracies can achieve (more) respect and recognition by other democracies by demonstrating their resolve in denigrating or fighting autocracies; in other words, honour-producing efforts can be used to increase one's prestige among comparable power monopolies.[7]

---

7 This is a possibility, not an absolute given. If democratic states see their rational, economic benefits enhanced by, e.g.for example, trade deals with non-democratic states, they will often prefer to follow that tack rather than idealistically augmenting their prestige. This is the case when Western powers interact with, say, Saudi Arabia to

Signs of Honour and Prestige, Historically and in Different States

Whether states seek honour, prestige or both, the signs and representations will vary according to the history of a given state, its size and significance vis-à-vis other states, its power resources and ambitions, the strength of its economy or some other factor. Basically, each state defines for itself what counts as significant for its self-respect and pride. Kagan (1997) is right to point out that 'honour includes such elements as the search for fame and glory; the desire to escape shame, disgrace, and embarrassment; the wish to avenge a wrong and thereby restore one's reputation; the determination to behave in accordance with certain moral ideals'. However, exactly *what* constitutes 'fame and glory' or *what* is perceived as embarrassing to a state varies a lot. For some states, fame and glory are tied to the acceptance by others of their international power, for the sake of which they are willing to go to war; for others, successes in sports or academic pursuits will suffice. For some, it is perceived as a historical blemish that the territory they once controlled has been diminished, and therefore they continuously advertise their irredentist claims (or desires) (Hungary); whereas other states in similar situations convert the same fact into a question of contemporary strength ('Little Denmark' on top of the welfare pyramid). Some attach great value to the prestige of their banking institutions and feel embarrassment when they fail (Switzerland); others symbolically prioritise having their own currency though the benefits are marginal, if not non-existent (Sweden; Denmark). The democratic order is a point of honour for some (particularly states with a somewhat different historical record – e.g. Germany, Japan), while others regard it as a threat to the state (China, North Korea). The six examples cited above demonstrate that the significance attached to various signs differs quite a lot across time and space, but also that 'such surface variations often conceal a fundamental similarity or even identity' (Kagan, 1997), that is, that all states lay great store by their honour and self-respect and will go to great lengths to defend them. They all keep lists of national heroes, they all commemorate past successes and they all envisage a bright future for the power of the state and the service of its people.

****

---

secure the procurement of oil deliveries. Hence, it is not true, as Kagan (1997) argues, that 'power is *never* pursued for itself' (italics in the original), but sometimes power *is* pursued for non-material reasons, or for reasons of power that are viewed as contributing to the international status of the state or the domestic respect of politicians among their electorates. See further below.

The pre-democratic world order (roughly prior to WWI) was dominated by colonial empires, or by ambitions to build colonial empires. As several commentators have pointed out, the Scramble for Africa was not per se a question of economic benefits for the European colonisers, but of the power to control territorial possessions.[8] Britain and France pursued different strategies, while Germany in particular had to make do with the sorry remains and consequently felt left out of the good company. The embarrassment this caused – a blemish to its national honour – was in no small way a contributing factor in the build-up to WWI, whilst Britain and France were able to bask in the relatively short-lived glory of their global possessions. Overall, the colonial empires were more concerned with their honour than their international prestige. The interwar years marked a kind of transition. Modern democracies and international institutions were created out of the rubble of colonial power ambitions; and although the pursuit of 'honour' by Churchill and de Gaulle in the face of the Nazi regime (and its ambitions for a vindication of the German humiliation in WWI) might indicate a continuation of colonial thinking, it nevertheless paved the way to a post-WWII order, where the honour and prestige of like-minded democracies entered into a new kind of relationship.

Obviously, this would not have happened without the power of the United States which, as the new global hegemon, called the shots during and after WWII and presaged the end of both the British and the French colonial empires in the decades to come. They both had to come to terms with the humiliation of the Suez Crisis (Hitchcock, 2018; Kingseed, 1995), and while Britain compensated by building the illusion of a 'special relationship' with the world power, France did its utmost to stay at the forefront of building the new Europe, the EEC and trying to keep Britain out. Gradually, the old-school colonial honour ambitions were replaced – or at least modified – by (varying) ambitions to amass national prestige in an international order dominated by the Americans. Idealistically formulated, this could be interpreted as follows: 'The victorious nations of the Great War were themselves democracies, dependent for their legitimacy on the support of the whole

---

8 In many ways, this struggle was illogical, to the point of negativity: it was basically a question of keeping the others from dominating stretches of land rather than of positive results from doing this yourself. Obviously, the colonisers nevertheless imagined that their control of different parts of Africa would yield not just strategic benefits but, eventually and down the line, economic advantages as well. Hence, South Africa and its gold mines served as the prime example of the economic value of colonisation and soon became the core area of contestation (the Boer War). See Pakenham, 1992, and https://www.newworldencyclopedia.org/entry/Scramble_for_Africa.

people [...]. War itself, in the new conception, was believed to be *morally wrong* [...]. Democracy, by contrast, was right and good in itself and also a force for peace' (Kagan, 1997). This utopia does not imply the death of the honour concept, however, which survived unscathed in the Cold War with the Soviets – the newfound absolute enemy – and theoretically in the notion of 'just wars' (Mosely, n.d.).[9]

Prestige and National Grandeur

Democratic states were thus faced with a new situation regarding their power, sovereignty and self-respect. The international order under American control compelled them to relativise the honour concept (and the aggressive, exclusivist methods it implies) and to accept achieving recognition and respect in more amicable ways. This is not to say that national grandeur was excluded as a goal in international affairs, but it had to be sought in more roundabout ways that were seen fit for democratic and peace-loving states, that is, diplomatically, through negotiations and political treaties, or it might be found in the substitute fields of sports, academic achievements and 'welfare' rankings. Kant's 'perpetual peace' (see below and Chapter 3) and the illusion that democracies never go to war against each other saw a revival, and the pursuit of national honour was relegated to the field of symbolics.[10]

In the midst of all this, the father of the 'Realist School', Hans Morgenthau, insisted that states still pursue interests and that prestige must take second place to the 'primary objective': 'The policy of prestige has two possible ultimate objectives: prestige for its own sake, or much more frequently, prestige in support of a policy of the status quo or of imperialism [...] it is rarely the primary objective of foreign policy [...] whose ultimate objectives are not the reputation for power but the substance of power [...] a policy of prestige attains its very triumph when it gives the nation pursuing it such a reputation for power as to enable it to forgo the actual employment of the instrument of

---

9   Further on this issue, see the section on 'Democratic vs dictatorial rule' below.
10 This is not the place to embark on the complex discussion about 'the long peace' following WWII, which constitutes the basis for the illusion. Suffice it to say that to this author, the relative absence of wars seems to stem rather from the military hegemony of the United States, which has made the 'war option' for others a non-rational and even suicidal path, rather than the spread and consolidation of the democratic state form. Moreover, the 'rule' is not without 'exceptions': when, for instance, the United States chose to intervene in Chile in 1973, overturning the democratically elected Allende regime, it demonstrated both the illusory nature of 'perpetual peace' between democracies and the reason other democracies do not dare overstep the same red line.

power' (Morgenthau, 1949, 55–57). Needless to say, Morgenthau obliquely expressed the viewpoint (and ambitions) of the American hegemon – the only state that did not have to abandon neither its absolute power ambitions nor the honour concept. Here, the 'substance of power' lent it prestige and honour to such an extent that it could hope to do without actually deploying its power resources: 'When enemies believe that a (!) country will use its military power, often it won't have to; the fear of a country's willingness to act decisively can deter aggression' (Thornton, 2017). The rest, however, were left with symbols of power, residual prestige and celebrations of past grandeur.

Domestic Benefits of International Prestige

The change from the pursuit of honour and glory in warlike encounters to that of seeking (and sometimes achieving) prestige among like-minded entities did not come without significant benefits for democratic states. Norway can point to its gigantic oil fund accumulated through offshore drilling in the North Sea or to its successes in winter skiing events; Switzerland prides itself on the strength of its economy, while staying formally aloof from the EU; Germany boosts its self-respect by celebrating its democratic institutions and the modesty of its population, in spite of its real power; England is proud of its Premier League, the international ranking of its universities and the cultural legacy it has bequeathed to the world; Denmark refers to its culinary feats and its folk high-school tradition; Brazil rides high on its World Cup successes; France takes pride in its intelligentsia, the Tour de France and its Force de Frappe; and nearly all states, especially the smaller ones, celebrate when their leaders are invited to the White House, which in their view confirms their international importance and boosts the pride of their citizens and their media;[11] and so on. All countries have areas where they excel and where they may gather international brownie points – international prestige (if they sometimes fail to realise this goal, it is perceived as humiliating). The real benefits of this kind of honour, however, have to do with its consequences domestically.

This is where the link between prestige, democracy and national identity reveals its real strength. The more international prestige a country can show

---

11 See for instance the mention in the Danish daily Politiken (24 May 2023) of Mette Frederiksen, the Danish prime minister's long-awaited invitation to join Joe Biden in the White House on 5 June 2023 (Astrup, 2023).

Danish political journalists breathed an audible sigh of relief and immediately started speculating if this might be the first step towards her takeover of Jens Stoltenberg's job as secretary general of NATO!

for itself, the more it will tend to boost the pride of its citizens, and the easier it becomes for national politicians to harvest the support of the electorate for the state and government. It is not necessary to wage wars or engage in bitter territorial conflicts with other states in order to increase popularity – this kind of 'honour' is widely regarded as old hat. Winning the World Cup in soccer, or a Nobel Prize, or making the Forbes 100 list, or boasting a number of three-star Michelin restaurants, or topping the ranking of the 'happiest populations' will all do the job. The job being to weld the state and people into one while giving citizens their fill of imagined gratification and leaving the business of managing the state's affairs to elected politicians. The admiration of others (real or imagined) works wonders in this regard.

It would naturally be desirable (so most politicians would no doubt think) if states could all show more real power for themselves, but, sadly, history has constructed the world of nations in such a way that it is strictly hierarchically organised, and only a few states can pride themselves on the ownership of the most awe-inspiring power symbols. For that reason, others have to bandwagon with these states (NATO),[12] try to stay neutral or non-aligned (India) or challenge the dominance of the hegemon while trying to acquire the same resources (Russia, China, North Korea). In other words, when push comes to shove, everything seems to hinge on the possession of (a maximum number of) *nuclear weapons*. This is also where prestige reverts back to questions of honour and international relations reveal their ugly face.

Nuclear Weapons, Honour and Prestige

War – belligerent encounters between states – has always loomed large in the search of nations for power and prestige and in the scholarly literature about this endeavour.[13] For the same reason, the possession of awe-inspiring and powerful military resources has historically played a prominent (symbolic) role. Barry O'Neill (2002, 1) correctly diagnosed this kind of effort as follows:

> In the siege warfare of medieval times, a central weapon was the artillery bombard, a wide-mouthed cannon used to fire stones against a castle's walls. During the 1400's some European powers wanted a bombard of awe-inspiring size. France had the Dule Grillet and Scotland the Mons Meg, which could hurl a 330-pound ball for two miles. They were

---

12 See for instance the analysis in Jakobsen et al, 2018, which reveals the extent to which Denmark and Norway have sought international prestige by supporting the United States in security matters and military operations.
13 See Markey, 1999.

impressive but impractical – bulky and vulnerable to being captured in a retreat [...]. A century later, large sea powers insisted on a warship displacing over 1000 tons: Scotland built the Great Michael, England the Harry Grace à Dieu, France the Grand FranHois, Sweden had the Elefant, and Portugal the São João. '[P]restige insisted on size,' the military historian J.R. Hale commented [...], adding that the money would have been better spent on several smaller ships.

Today, this kind of role has been taken over by nuclear weapons. They are formidable, all-destructive and can be deployed on land, at sea and in the air – and possibly soon in space as well. They are strategic and tactical, intermediate-range and intercontinental. They clinched WWII. Without being actually launched, they undoubtedly decided the outcome of the Cold War too. Becoming a nuclear power is hence the ultimate dream of all states, and even better if you are able to display as many and as powerful nuclear weapons as can be imagined. O'Neill knows this too:

> Some countries have sought prestige through nuclear weapons. To Charles de Gaulle, the issue of a French bomb was not just military strategy but 'Will France remain France?' [...] According to Mao, China built its bomb in part for international status [...]. Walsh (1997) documented Australia's little-known nuclear quest during the 1960s, and saw the military's motive as standing proud beside their colleagues in the United States and Britain. According to many analysts, Saddam Hussein's program is aimed at gaining the prestige to make him a regional leader, and Iran's activities have a corresponding motive. Indian leaders expected that their first explosion in 1974 would enhance their country's prestige [...] and many predicted more benefits from the 1998 tests. Prestige is not the only motive for these weapons, of course, and in some cases of proliferation it may be absent, but it led India to acquire them even though the net consequence seems to have been a decrease in security. (ibid., 1–2)

For most countries, however, becoming a nuclear power remains a pipe dream. The actual possession of a nuclear arsenal is strictly limited to fewer than 10 states, which all try to prevent further nuclear proliferation. Some of these states have even come into possession of their nuclear arsenal illegitimately (North Korea) or clandestinely (Israel), and the rest constitute a pecking order of symbolic power, with the United States and Russia at the top, followed by China, the United Kingdom and France and with India and

Pakistan trailing far behind. The former five for that reason are permanent members of the UN Security Council and bask in the power and prestige this status gives them: the ultimate badge of honour, the international recognition that they wield more power than all the rest.

In one sense, this is an oddity. If normal parlance, political discourse and many scholarly contributions are to be believed, nuclear weapons are not there to be used but only to *represent* the power of a state, deter aggression and inspire fear. For the actual use of them in war would allegedly be counterproductive, since it would wipe out the human race, civilisation as we know it, and hence the nuclear powers themselves. In other words, nuclear weapons supposedly only serve a symbolic, defensive purpose; they are 'prestige symbols […] ideal prototypes' (O'Neill, 2002). This at least is the take of idealists, moralists and original embracers of the 'just war' concept, who mainly see the danger of nuclear use in instances of miscommunication or personal mistakes on the part of political leaders.[14]

On the other hand, however, this approach might be too good to be true. For though nuclear weapons might be seen to represent a 'moral paradox', and 'are magnitudes more destructive than even the most powerful conventional weapons, this does not immediately render them unusable under traditional Just War constraints' (Lytwyn, 2018).[15] Admittedly, 'early weapon systems lacked accuracy', but the world today is a different place and the world power takes another view: 'Advocates of nuclear disarmament, such as ICAN,[16] work to delegitimize and ban nuclear weapons. In contrast, the United States strives to preserve their legitimacy by reserving nuclear weapons for extreme circumstances and even then applying the law of armed conflict when considering their possible use. As former United States Strategic Command (USSTRATCOM) commander General Robert Kehler recently noted, "the law of war governs the use of U.S. nuclear weapons. Nuclear options and orders are no different in this regard than any other weapon"' (ibid.).

---

14 A few 'structural realists' support this argument as well. See e.g. Martin, 2013.
15 For a detailed review of the US strategy concerning nuclear weapons, see Department of Defense, 2018. For an overview of US policies, strategies and dilemmas in regard to nuclear weapons during the Cold War period (deterrence, flexible response, mutual assured destruction, 'stars wars' and anti-missile defences, etc.), see the account in Holsti, 1991, 286–295.
16 The International Campaign to Abolish Nuclear Weapons states: 'Nuclear deterrence makes nuclear use more likely because the threat of use of nuclear weapons must be credible, and so the nuclear armed states are always poised to launch nuclear weapons' (ICAN, n.d.).

So, both international law and a flexible Just War notion actually legitimise the use of nuclear weapons, especially since the arsenal is much more elaborate than it used to be:

> Critically, the Just War tradition avoids imposing a standard that all civilian casualties must be avoided (something no country could achieve without the risk of losing an otherwise legitimate war). Instead, the tradition levies a more realistic standard that collateral damage must be avoided to the extent feasible while in pursuit of legitimate military objectives. Charles Dunlap, a former Staff Judge Advocate at USSTRATCOM, highlights the ability of nuclear weapons to be used discriminately, noting that 'by reducing weapon yield, improving accuracy through delivery system selection, employing multiple small weapons (as opposed to a single, large device), adjusting the height of burst, and offsetting the desired ground zero, collateral damage can be minimized consistent with military objectives'.
>
> The international community itself has not seen fit to judge all potential nuclear weapons use as disproportionate. (ibid.)

Thus, the nuclear arsenal has been emancipated from the constraints of morality and political philosophy; it can be used. The superpower has moved miles away from the stalemate of the Cold War, when the arsenals on either side made the outcome of a nuclear encounter difficult to calculate. Possessing nuclear weapons is not *just* a question of international prestige and national honour (though also that), but centrally a question of power. If the moralists were right, it would indeed be the first time monopolies of power had squandered billions of dollars on weapons that would be solely there for symbolic reasons. It would also defy any normal logic: how can weapons be seen as a threat if they are not there to be used?

Clearly, though, this does not eliminate the prestige angle entirely. Even though the likelihood of, for example, India, Israel or Pakistan actually resorting to the use of their nuclear arsenal is minimal, it does heighten their prestige internationally; the mere fact that they might use it in extreme circumstances increases their deterrence. This, in fact, also applies to France and the United Kingdom, which are unlikely to use their nuclear capacity outside NATO – meaning without the go-ahead of the United States. Russia and China are different; here, existential threats to the two states might well lead to the use of 'the bomb'.[17] Which of course is also why the two nations

---

17 What constitutes an existential threat is something that each state defines for itself, which is what makes the actual use of nuclear weapons hard to predict.

are seen not just as competitors but also as enemies by the United States and the West – for it cannot be because their economic systems militate against that of the Western world, and also their lack of democracy is not a believable reason (though it is often that which is cited). In that case, it would be hard to explain how Saudi Arabia, other Middle Eastern states, most states on the African continent, and so on, always seem to avoid being categorised and stigmatised as enemies. Even the massive support of Ukraine would be inexplicable. Nevertheless, let me take a closer look at the question of honour and prestige in light of the democracy/dictatorship divide.

Democratic vs Dictatorial Rule[18]

Democracy is a system in which 'the citizens get to decide who deserves to rule them', whereas 'dictatorship is a rigid form of government in which people are not given the liberties they could otherwise get in the democratic form of government'; here 'the head of the state is not elected by them'; 'the word of the dictator is law' (Basics, 2023). Phrased differently, it is not a question of whether or not the rulers rule, but whether or not the rule people are subjected to has been legitimised by themselves. In democracies, people are allowed to decide *who* should rule them, but not *what* the contents of the rule are going to be. In dictatorships, on the other hand, rulers have grabbed power all on their own, without asking for permission and without giving the people the chance (liberty/right) to replace them with other rulers at regular intervals. Democracy has for this reason, somewhat cynically, been described as 'the worst form of government – except for all the others that have been tried' (Churchill). Other democratic representatives find more jubilant tones: 'Democracy is not only about elections: it is also about creating and encouraging the building blocks of an open and fair society: the rule of law, protection of minorities, strong political parties, liberty, a free media, a strong role for civil society and action against corruption' (Millett, 2014). However, democracy 'is a process not an event. There will inevitably be bumps along the road. And it will mean continually adjusting to new demands for better ways to deliver governments that can govern effectively. Evolution is better than revolution. And peaceful protest is better than rebellion' (ibid.).

Hence, democracy is about 'effective government', which is met by 'peaceful protest' rather than violent rebellion. It is a mature kind of rule, which

---

18 This section primarily concentrates on democracies and their views of dictatorships. An independent investigation of honour in non-democratic states is beyond the scope of this chapter.

has realised that it is wise to let the citizens themselves decide the 'who', if the politicians – always constrained by laws that they have themselves put in place – decide the 'what'.

The difference between the two forms of government might sound modest, but of course it is not. Democratic politicians take pride in the fact that they have won the confidence of the electorate and have been chosen to lead their people, even if their leadership is often met with protest and disgruntlement – and sometimes by new elections and a change of government. Also, they routinely congratulate leaders in other countries when they have been elected to 'serve' by their citizens, though the congratulatory notes will invariably reflect the specific interest the senders have in the receiving power holders.

So, being a democratically elected leader is no doubt a question of prestige in the international world of politics. But is it also a question of 'honour' in such measure that states are willing to wage wars on that account? Are dictatorships, that is, non-democratic governments, such an eyesore that this fact in itself would be sufficient to enter into armed conflict? Is democracy a question of life and death for states and their citizens, in other words?

The examples briefly referred to at the end of the previous section would suggest no. However, many scholars, public intellectuals, political actors and ordinary citizens would disagree. For instance, Kagan (1997) argues that '(t)he 20th century [...] introduced yet a new sense of honour into international relations'. 'The struggle [following WWI] would be between increasingly democratic states on the one hand and, on the other, tyrannies or dictatorships of one form or another. The victorious nations in the Great War were themselves democracies, dependent for their legitimacy on the support of the whole people, and this circumstance gave birth to a new set of ideas as to what was honorable in the conduct of nations.'

Now Britain, France and the United States might, in various degrees, be said to be democracies at the time, but Russia most certainly was not. And worse, this says little about the reasons state alliances chose to sacrifice millions of their citizens on the battlefield. WWI was basically a struggle about colonies and empires, and the fact that it ended up supporting nation states, self-determination and the gradual process of decolonisation was an 'unintended consequence' seen from the point of view of both losers and victors in the war, with one exception: the United States. Hence, Kagan can proudly embrace the superior take of the real winner when he declares that 'Woodrow Wilson was thus not speaking for himself alone when he said that a crucial aim of the Great War had been the defense and extension of democracy'. However, neither was this a crucial aim to start with, nor was it the central objective of the United States. For all the original states involved, it hinged on the possession or non-possession of colonial stretches of land, and for the

United States, it was a matter of ending the colonial system, which stood in the way of American interests in the world and the American domination of the world. The Treaty of Versailles and Wilson's 14 points, which codified national independence and the self-determination of peoples, constituted a weapon in the American arsenal aimed at world hegemony, but of course it lent to this mundane purpose a higher value and a more high-falutin' discourse: prestige, rights and morality. 'Political elites in the democracies [...] would henceforth need to deal with a public opinion that [...] firmly linked the need to resist aggression with the concept of moral honour' (Kagan, 1997).

Kagan continues by highlighting the classic example that is frequently used to underpin this approach, that is, that of Italy's invasion of Abyssinia (Ethiopia) in 1935 and the British and French reactions to the attack. 'Before the Great War it would have been extremely unlikely that a European assault on a weak African nation of no particular value or interest to other European powers would have provoked a meaningful reaction. And even now there was little sentiment within the British government for a strong stand against Italy. Some argued for a prudent, 'realist' policy.' However, '[b]y 1935, many British felt they could not ignore the commitment to resist aggression, *whether or not* their country was capable of resisting it effectively' (my emphasis). The subsequent Hoare-Laval agreement (between Britain and France, accepting the Italian invasion) was hence 'greeted in Britain by an outburst of angry disapproval and was widely condemned as a reward for aggression [...]. Hoare was forced to resign'.

Similarly, Neville Chamberlain met resistance when he tried his hand at a policy of appeasement with Hitler, abandoning support of Czechoslovakia and Poland in 1938 and 1939. The parliamentary opposition (Labour and Liberals) argued vehemently against this, allegedly 'not on strategic grounds, but on the score of morality and ideology' (Correlli Barnett, *pace* Kagan). Churchill, on the other hand, 'formulated a policy of resistance that accurately reflected the feelings of most of the British people, who preferred the risks and suffering of a terrible war to the dishonor of a shameful peace' (ibid.). In other words, morality vanquished interest, 'honour' surpassed 'realism', popular feelings guided political action, democracy stood up against fascism.

Now, does this idyllic picture actually portray the full truth of the matter? Let's take a step back. Britain and France were still colonial empires that had been used to taking control, issuing orders, ruling other countries and taking military action whenever this was deemed necessary. They were now faced with other European powers (Italy and Germany) which conducted a policy of revanchism and expansion, which might not have been directed against them in the first place, but which obviously involved political and economic risks, threatening their dominant position in Europe and possibly the colonies as well. From the point of view of national interest, realism or what have you, they were therefore faced with an uncomfortable choice: either to let the aggressors have their way and only react when the 'motherland' was directly attacked, or to take preemptive action while trying to defend their dominant positions as powerful colonial empires. Britain eventually chose the latter strategy, while France, initially at least, opted for a policy of collaboration with Nazi Germany.

It is unsurprising that Britain's reaction became wrapped in moralism and ideology, which was facilitated by the fact that in this case, the country was not the aggressor and was able to count on the support of the majority of the population. A 'peace' struck with the Germans would, however, not just be perceived as 'shameful', but would in actual fact pose a threat to the political, military and economic position of the UK in Europe as well as the world; in other words, to British interests and the British conception of its national selfhood. Hoare and Chamberlain, like Pétain in France, chose to collaborate with the fascists, in the hope that their word could be trusted and that they would be content with the spoils they had so far obtained. Churchill and de Gaulle, on the other hand, analysed the situation more clearly and staked their reputation on resisting the fascist aggressors, while simultaneously referring to democracy and national honour as the staple and objective of their endeavours. The successful outcome was, of course, not a done deal and would not have been achieved without the Americans and the Soviets. On the other hand, as Kagan correctly points out, 'Britain's example has had a great influence on Western and especially on American attitudes ever since. The "Munich analogy" was, of course, a major force in shaping the policy of the United States in its confrontation with the Soviet Union' (1997). This confrontation was 'certainly a contest for power', but 'no less important was the conflict of values and ideas, in which questions of honor were inextricably entwined' (ibid.).

It would be a mistake, however, to see these two parts (power and honour) as parallel objectives that carry each their own independent weight. The power contest was unquestionably the primary reason for the American belligerence towards the USSR; and 'honour' constituted the ideological wrapping, the factor 'that went beyond a conception of their material interest' (Kagan), and an objective that matched both the passions of the American people and public opinion in the West. The 'happy' outcome – the breakdown of Soviet-style Communism – 'could never have been achieved merely by the pursuit of what experts considered to be our practical national interests' (Kagan, 1997). The identification between the world of (national) politics and the world of political scholarship, which is evident in Kagan's (representative) use of the first-person plural pronoun above, makes for a fitting transition to the next section.[19]

Scholarly Fallacies

I have already touched on the most significant fallacies of the scholarship on states' honour and prestige. The following is meant to briefly summarise and explain recurrent errors and pitfalls. They subdivide into the 'what' section and the 'why' section, that is, on the one hand the descriptive errors and on the other their underlying causality. There are five points in the former, while merely one in the latter. My contention is, thus, that all the five major errors derive from the same uniform cause. Obviously, not all contributions contain the same fallacies, and a few manage to avoid them all. However, most articles and books on the honour and prestige of modern states, in political science or political philosophy, derive their theoretical missteps from the following package.

The 'what' section

- *The personalisation error.* This was mentioned already in the introduction to this chapter. States are treated as if they were human beings, whose honour has been molested and who therefore do their utmost to vindicate their moral ego and avoid public humiliation. Raymond Aron (1962/1973) expressed the analogy clearly: 'Political units have their *amour-propre*, as people do'.[20] Humans are out to defend their 'good name', or that of their family. In early modern times, this often took the form of duels between members of the aristocracy. Modern states, on the other hand, are monopolies of power, institutions much less sensitive to irrational, personalised insult, but, as sovereign entities, used to having their

---

19 It is important that three components of state elites' honour-seeking ambitions – the international, the domestic and the psychological, all contribute their individual parts to the overall picture but play different roles. The international delivers the basis: striving for honour would not exist without the interplay of different states and state actors. The domestic constitutes the pragmatic element: state elites extract electoral advantage from their successes on the international stage. But psychologically, 'honour seeking' is not a rational strategic game for politicians, but is driven by their ideologically rooted vanity, their 'amour-propre' (Rousseau, 1762/2017).
20 See also O'Neill, 2003, 1: 'National states treat each other as if they were persons, exchanging insults, issuing challenges, and retaliating against wrongs in the name of 'national' honour'.

way in the domestic arena. To achieve something similar in external matters, they have set up an array of different instruments to protect and extend their interests: financial, diplomatic, political, military and so on. Only when these instruments of power are no longer sufficient or successful, and they feel degraded or misrepresented, are honour and moralism called on as the ultimate weapons. Then, but only then, do they represent themselves as insulted or humiliated characters in the morality play of states. Scholars buy into that narrative far too willingly: shame, humiliation and the search for honour are perceived as natural and ubiquitous reactions, be it by persons, groups or states. This is an integral part of the moralisation and personalisation of power monopolies. See further the last error below.

- *The banalisation error.* This was basically dealt with in the section on nuclear weapons and international prestige, which is also where the error is most blatant and most serious. It would seem that the more frightening and destructive the weapons, the more they are just meant to symbolise power, not to be used. Here, scholars often take the perspective of the United States and generalise it, whether knowingly or not. Following Khong (2019), E. H. Carr and Robert Gilpin, for instance, write variously that 'if your strength is recognized, you can generally achieve your aims without having to use it [military power]' (Carr), and 'in the [...] resolution of conflicts among states there is actually little use of overt force' (Gilpin, 1981, 31). And nuclear weapons, according to Allison (2017), actually contribute – not to threatening the destruction of the globe – but the opposite: 'The advent of nuclear weapons has introduced an important restraint against major power war' (244). So, we do not have to fear a nuclear disaster. Many scholars of international relations would agree. Nuclear weapons are principally symbolic, and should they actually come to be used, the technological advances are such that they will only be used tactically, with circumspection and without resorting to anything resembling 'mutual assured destruction'. On the other hand, so the argument runs, what dictatorships like Russia or North Korea might be plotting is less certain, which is why they should not be allowed to possess such frightening weapons; the honour of the free world hinges on their containment. Hence, the West needs an overpowering arsenal of nuclear weapons, which can keep the dictators from using theirs.
- *The democracy error.* This is, in a sense, the most tragic and consequential pitfall. It constitutes a 'degraded' version of Kant's idea of 'perpetual peace' (Kant, 1795/1903), which was hedged around with multiple ifs and buts and (according to Kant) hinged on the utopia of republics (later democracies) willingly and gradually organising their intercourse as a

'federation of free states'. Even by Kant himself, this was seen as a fragile ideal, which was difficult to realise.[21] Contemporary political moralists are cruder and more optimistic: democracies are peace-loving, try to avoid war and don't go to war against each other; they only engage in 'just wars' when they are forced into them; and their honour and international prestige are linked to their civilised, diplomatic, non-belligerent behaviour vis-à-vis each other. Some certainly disagree, but the celebration of the democratic order is endless. Nevertheless, democracies are (also) monopolies of power, which, due to their national interests, sometimes belie even their democratic, pacifist idealism (the United States in Chile 1973; the United Kingdom against Argentina in the Falklands War); they may be discounted as 'real' democracies when they do, or are listed as exceptions to the rule. For the developed democracies of the 'First World,' it is, in any case, fortuitous that they are, numerically, in a clear minority in the community of states. First, they have more or less eliminated the traditional cause of war amongst them, that is, territorial disputes,[22] and, more importantly, there are multiple dictatorships left which pose a threat to the free world and are hence honourable targets of just wars.

- *The moralism error.* This fallacy is the direct corollary of the former: in brief, its message is that moral arguments and concerns often annul or override state interests. Realists are apparently mistaken; (democratic) states are humane constructions concerned with the softer side of politics and bent on preserving their good name both as regards their peoples and their fellow statesmen beyond their borders. Political normativity

---

21 For instance, the conclusion of Kant's 'second definitive article' runs like this: 'For states, in their relation to one another, there can be, according to reason, no other way of advancing from that lawless condition which unceasing war implies, than by giving up their savage lawless freedom, just as individual men have done, and yielding to the coercion of public laws. Thus they can form a State of nations (*civitas gentium*), one, too, which will be ever increasing and would finally embrace all the peoples of the earth. States, however, in accordance with their understanding of the law of nations, by no means desire this, and therefore reject *in hypothesi* what is correct *in thesi*. Hence, instead of the positive idea of a world-republic, if all is not to be lost, only the negative substitute for it, a federation averting war, maintaining its ground and ever extending over the world may stop the current of this tendency to war and shrinking from the control of law. But even then there will be a constant danger that this propensity may break out' (Kant, 1795/1991).
22 This does not mean that there are no other potential reasons left that might lead to wars between developed democracies, only that power and domination no longer rest on territorial hegemony, but rather on economic, financial and military supremacy.

is, now, 'that war is increasingly seen as an unacceptable means to settle disputes' (Khong, 2019). Kagan agrees: 'War itself, in the new conception, was believed to be *morally* wrong' (1997; emphasis in the original), while adding: ' [...] its causes connected with the aggressiveness natural to authoritarian and despotic regimes'. Peoples' influence on politicians in democracies allegedly links 'the need to resist aggression with the concept of moral honor' (ibid.). This fact also helps to explain the Cold War and American resistance to the USSR: 'Not only American security but also decency and honor argued for its containment' (ibid.). Otherwise, 'the American people would [not] have accepted military service, higher taxes [...], and a permanent European alliance' (ibid.). The Realists were proved wrong – in more senses than one. Not just did morality prevail – it was also successful: 'To the confusion of the realists, Ronald Reagan's determined efforts to build up American defenses and consign "the evil empire" to dust was followed neither by American economic implosion nor by suicidal war but by the collapse of the Soviet Union' (ibid.). In a manner of speaking, Reagan was a better realist than the Realists: 'To attempt to exclude [moral values] from consideration is the height of fantasy, and *the opposite of realism*' (ibid.; my italics). National interests are best served if morality is properly taken into account. Realism has been resuscitated, and the central role of popular sentiments in international politics has been restored.

Now, as should have been made apparent, I am not arguing that morality plays no role in the conduct of state affairs, but that it rarely plays an *independent* role. Sometimes, however, it does override the 'normal' objectives of states, but that is precisely when politicians seriously consider the war option, and not when they shy away from war because they see it as 'an unacceptable means to settle disputes'.

- *The anthropological-historical error.* This is a more serious version of the first error, the personalisation fallacy. Its basis is that all power ambitions, all modes of politics, whether realist or idealist, cynical or moral, derive from that intangible source, *human nature*, with all its multiple complexities. Whether we go back to the ancient authors (notably Aristotle and Thucydides), to Machiavelli, Hobbes, Rousseau, Kant or Morgenthau, we find the same assumption. Politics basically derives from personal ambitions, vanity, reason or emotion, incompatible private volitions, self-interest and the urge to dominate, the desire to be admired and respected, or (for some) the moral voice that impels humans to restrain their competitive drive, behave in a more civilised manner and accept a social contract. If war and anarchy are to be avoided, state and politics – the rule of law – are a necessary evil, even a blessing in disguise. In *Politics*

Among Nations, Hans Morgenthau (1949, 4) summarised this approach in an exemplary manner: '[h]uman nature, in which the [objective] laws of politics have their roots, has not changed since the classical philosophies of China, India, and Greece endeavoured to discover these laws'. The precise contents of human nature, this essentialist anthropological constant, is a source of endless strife and disagreements among political philosophers, but the majority would buy into the proposition that this is the core issue underlying all politics (and society, including the economy). For the same reason, it is a straightforward matter to present past theories as if they were versions of contemporary realism,[23] or to transfer the *amour-propre* of individuals to the search for prestige among states. For there are humans everywhere and they are all motivated by similar ambitions for power, recognition and honour, not least in the anarchic area of international politics.

The 'why' section

All these fallacies might be explained with reference to chance, coincidence or subjective errors on the part of scholars. However, given their systematic repetitiveness, it is more likely that we should look for the reason elsewhere. In the following, I try to explain what in my view is the most likely cause, and as intimated above, there is basically only one, though it comes in different variations.

- *The partiality error*. Fundamentally, the underlying causality can be identified as the partiality, or bias, of the scholarly community. Political scholars take sides, identifying with the struggle and objectives of 'their own' statesmen, statesmen fighting for the democratic order, the free world, or 'their own' nation states. Also on this score, Donald Kagan is explicit and

---

23 'In the discipline of International Relations (IR), realism is a school of thought that emphasises the competitive and conflictual side of international relations. Realism's roots are often said to be found in some of humankind's earliest historical writings, particularly Thucydides' history of the Peloponnesian War, which raged between 431 and 404 BCE. Thucydides, writing over two thousand years ago, was not a "realist" because IR theory did not exist in named form until the twentieth century. However, when looking back from a contemporary vantage point, theorists detected many similarities in the thought patterns and behaviours of the ancient world and the modern world. They then drew on his writings, and that of others, to lend weight to the idea that there was a timeless theory spanning all recorded human history. That theory was named "realism"' (Antunes & Camisão, 2018).

difficult to misunderstand, possibly due to his well-known neo-conservative sympathies. His article from 1997, which I have cited liberally, was titled '*Our* Interests and *Our* Honor'. The plural pronoun is all-encompassing. It indicates the union of the author with the powers that be in their universal fight for 'the vindication of freedom and democracy' – a 'happy outcome [which] could never have been achieved merely by the pursuit if what experts considered to be our (!) practical national interests', but also, more narrowly, his identification with the *American* cause and the alleged 'commitment of Americans at large to values deeper and more humanly compelling than concern over economic and geopolitical advantage'. Kagan thus idealises the politics of the Western world and 'his own' nation and, in the same move, identifies with it; he takes sides. He allows feelings, in the form of moralism, to enter the objective world of political science and gives the struggle for the honour of the/his nation the thumbs-up.

- Kagan may be exceptionally direct and his preferences explicit, but he is far from alone. Twenty years later, Bruce Thornton, in 'Prestige as a Tool of Foreign Policy' (2017) – on the foreign policy of Donald Trump – talks about 'restoring our (!) country's damaged prestige' and basically builds the entire argument around the use of the moral 'we'. He refers to modern jihadism's 'perception of our hedonism and weakness, our foundations of straw', and urges that 'unless we persist in restoring our prestige with mind-concentrating force, these perceptions will continue to motivate our enemies, damage our national interests, and cost American lives' (ibid.). Of course, not all scholarly contributions are that easy to decipher, and academics regularly do their best to avoid such direct and open (moral) identification with their object of analysis. However, even Morgenthau reveals his preference when, for instance, he writes in *Politics Among Nations* that

> in the struggle for existence and power – which is, as it were, the raw material of the social world – what others think about us is as important as what we actually are. The image in the mirror of our fellows' minds (that is, our prestige), rather than the original, of which the image in the mirror may be but the distorted reflection, determines what we are as members of society. (1949, 86–87)

Admittedly, this is a somewhat different 'we', more oblique, more abstract, more theoretical, but nevertheless a 'we' that defines 'us' as 'members of society', which we all know is national and adorned with a state and its political leaders.

- The argument I offer is thus that the five errors all derive from the interested identification of political scholars with the order they live in, are members of, and feel they have a duty to defend. They allow morality and idealisation to enter the theoretical world by the back door, so to speak. Science and interest merge. This is most serious and consequential as regards the democracy error, but it is also noticeable when scholars downplay the seriousness of nuclear weapons or ascribe power and prestige to a universal humanity motive and thus, in a sense, take the state out of the equation. It must be added that the errors do not neutralise the insights, analytical conclusions, and theoretical advances otherwise present in scholarly contributions on honour and prestige; but they are no doubt limiting factors that must be borne in mind by the serious reader.

Conclusion

Thucydides saw fit to speak of prestige-motivated conflict in the fifth century BCE, and echoes of his wisdom could be heard at the flowering of Renaissance Italy, rising over the din of religious wars in England, and filtering through the dawn of the French Enlightenment. Indeed, political realists spanning a period of over two millennia have recognized prestige as an intrinsic interest of individuals and states. Today, however, mainstream international relations theory has dropped the prestige 'variable' from the political equation (Markey, 1999, 171).

Daniel Markey did his best to re-open the prestige issue in 1999, but alas, with limited success. The subject has since been at best marginal in IR studies, at worst neglected. Though Hans Morgenthau had not closed the door on the subject, after the collapse of the USSR, interest waned, and Markey knew why: 'Prestige is an instrumental end, not an intrinsic one' (ibid., 129). True, in IR studies this is mostly so, but only mostly. For when prestige becomes a matter of the honour of states, things start to change. When, in other words, the question is one that goes to the heart of a state's, a nation's, existential being, its survival and core identity, 'prestige' turns into something extremely intrinsic and significant. This is when heroism is in great demand and when economic and human sacrifices are not just required but also celebrated. Where the state is 'normally' the servant of the economy and its leading representatives, in war the relationship is turned upside down. The current war between Russia and Ukraine is ample evidence. Both do their utmost to defend their honour and represent the other side as the incarnation of immorality; their interest is no longer mainly economic but one that is imbricated with the identity and survival of the nation.[24] That the consequence is the death of hundreds of thousands of people and the destruction of natural environments, production sites and living quarters is of scant importance. For this is the collision of two power monopolies, not any family vendetta or individual act of revenge. Fighting for the national honour represents the very core of interstate relations. This will be the sole focus of Chapter 3.

---

24 'That the extreme case appears to be an exception does not negate its decisive character but confirms it all the more. [...] One can say that the exceptional case has an especially decisive meaning which exposes the core of the matter' (Schmitt, 1932/2007, 35). 'Even with the last few centuries' civilianization of Western governments, war has remained the defining activity of national states' (Tilly, 1992, 187).

Chapter 3

WAR, PEACE AND MORALITY: 10 THESES ON THE COST OF FREEDOM – AND A CASE STUDY OF THE WAR IN UKRAINE

The cost of freedom is always high, but Americans have always paid it. And one path we shall never choose, and that is the path of surrender, or submission.
(John F. Kennedy)

10 Theses

1.

The relationship between war and peace is complementary, not contradictory. Reasons of war are produced in peacetime. Peace is no antidote to war. Carl von Clausewitz realised as much in *On War* back in 1832:

> We say therefore War belongs not to the province of Arts and Sciences, but to the province of social life. It is a conflict of great interests which is settled by bloodshed, and only in that is it different from others. It would be better, instead of comparing it with any Art, to liken it to business competition, which is also a conflict of human interests and activities; and it is still more like State policy, which again, on its part, may be looked upon as a kind of business competition on a great scale. Besides, State policy is the womb in which War is developed, in which its outlines lie hidden in a rudimentary state, like the qualities of living creatures in their germs.[1]

---

1 Clausewitz, 1832/1976, Book 3, Chapter 3. The American pragmatist William James, some 80 years later, put the thought more crudely: 'Every up-to-date dictionary should say that "peace" and "war" mean the same thing, now *in posse,* now *in actu*. It may even reasonably be said that the intensely sharp competitive *preparation* for war by the

Stanley Hoffmann, following Rousseau, phrases the same insight differently, while turning a famous Clausewitz dictum on its head: 'peace treaties (are) nothing but stratagems [...], the continuation of war by other means' (1987, 34; see further the second thesis below). Kalevi J. Holsti also had an inkling: 'Peace then becomes the father of war' (1991, 353), but his 'then' marks an important caveat: 'peace settlements', in his view, may provide a means to alleviate and cope with 'issues' in the future, can allegedly help produce 'less war-prone international orders'. However, on the basis of Holsti's detailed analysis of 'armed conflicts and international order 1648–1989', peace does not strike the reader as a solution to the 'issue' of war, but at best as a temporary delaying factor, at worst as utopian idealism. In similar manner, Immanuel Kant's *Zum ewigen Frieden* (Kant, 1795/1903) – a hope for 'perpetual peace' that he pinned to republicanism in its ideal form, though not without significant hesitation and caveats – must be characterised as basically naïve. War and peace interchangeably define each other, each being the mirror reflection of the other. States involved in wars always do it in the name of peace; their troops are there to secure peace. Clausewitz again: 'A conqueror is always a lover of peace'.[2] NATO, too, is a peace-loving war alliance, its activities being purely defensive. In the preamble to its foundational document, the members of the North Atlantic Treaty Organization – the most formidable military alliance the world has seen – affirm their commitment 'to live in peace with all peoples and all governments', to preserve 'peace and security', and further (in Article 1) to 'settle any international disputes in which they may be involved by peaceful means in such a manner that international peace and security, and justice, are not endangered'. War is hardly mentioned, and where it is – only to be refuted. NATO will 'refrain in their international relations from the threat or use of force' (Article 1), but adds the rider 'in any manner inconsistent with the purposes of the United Nations'. Hence, Article 3 spells out, they 'will maintain and develop their individual and collective capacity to resist armed attack', and an 'armed attack against one or more of them in Europe or North America shall be considered an attack against them all' (Article 5).[3] The Treaty does not explain how living 'in peace with all peoples and all governments' can lead to an armed attack by all or some of these peoples and governments; it is simply taken for granted

---

nations is *the real war*, Permanent, unceasing; and that the battles are only a sort of public verification of the mastery gained during the "peace" interval' (James, 1911, 273–274).

2 Clausewitz, 1832/1976, Book 6, Chapter 5.
3 NATO, 1995.

that in spite of the most sincere (individual or organisational) efforts to maintain 'peace', 'war' can and will often be the result. International relations in peacetime engender the reasons for conflict and war.[4]

2.

The logical result of the first thesis is, as Clausewitz also knew, that war is the continuation of politics with other means – that is, other means of *power*.

> We see, therefore, that war is not merely an act of policy but a true political instrument, a continuation of political intercourse, carried on with other means. What remains peculiar to war is simply the peculiar nature of its means. War in general, and the commander in any specific instance, is entitled to require that the trend and designs of policy shall not be inconsistent with these means. That, of course, is no small demand; but however much it may affect political aims in a given case, it will never do more than modify them. The political object is the goal, war is the means of reaching it, and means can never be considered in isolation from their purpose.[5]

This well-known and generally accepted truism needs further scrutiny and some reservation, however. On the face of it, it might be taken to imply that politics remains unaltered but the instruments applied to effect it are different. War becomes just another compartment in the political toolbox, and there is a smooth, gradualist link between 'peace' and 'war'. This conception is mistaken. Although it is true that war *is* a political instrument and that the long-term goals of peace and war are the same, war nevertheless alters the relationship between the state and its citizens, the state and the economy, and (of course) the state and states on the opposite side in rather fundamental ways. As some of the following theses will explain, the apparent 'exception' which war represents tends to annul or downplay the 'civic' goals of 'normal' state activities and move the state itself to the centre of things. 'Democracy, individual liberty and the rule of law' (NATO Preamble), which are top of the league for most (Western) states, are all severely limited or completely done away with in a situation where the very existence of the state is at risk. Now, 'honour' takes over, and the private concerns and affairs of individuals become submerged in the preparation for and conduct of war. Citizens turn

---

4 For reasons, see Thesis no 3 below.
5 *On War*, Book 1, Chapter 1, 24th paragraph.

into soldiers, and the economy becomes an instrument for the state – not vice versa.

Now, this naturally assumes that we are talking about industrialised democracies and not pre-democratic empires, fascist states or some other kind of autocratic regimes, where individuals are not equipped with democratic liberties, and where the state (often personified as one individual), rather than seeing itself as a servant of economic interests, represents the be-all and end-all of political and economic endeavours. Obviously, early nineteenth-century Prussia, which Clausewitz represented, was not a developed democracy, nor was its immediate opponent, Napoleonic France. Prussia was a militarised kingdom, which finally came out of the wars against France victorious and added significantly to its territorial and economic reach following the Congress of Vienna in 1815. In this historical perspective, Clausewitz was no doubt right in emphasising that 'war is the continuation of politics with other means'; no hiatus having to be understood between the roles of the state prior to and during the war. Or differently put, peacetime was a state of militarised wait for the next warring conflict, a state of permanent emergency and preparation for the next exchange of arms. It was pretty obvious in those times, despite Kant and his notion of permanent peace, that there was no rupture between peace and war.

This is less clear today, where peace movements and organisations abound, states are rooted in the popular will, and even NATO can present itself as a peaceful alliance (pitted against all the evil dictatorships that still exist). This is the place to consider the present-day *reasons* for war and why the relationship between peace and war is (still) complementary.

3.

It is a common liberalist assumption that trade and interdependence breed peace, because the gains of trade (some say *free* trade) will trump the costs of war. Patrick J. McDonald summarises:

> A number of explanations have been proposed. Trade promotes peace through communication and transnational ties that increase understanding among societies and the potential for cooperation. While expanding an international web of commerce through specialization, trade makes war less likely by increasing the cost of severing such economic links. Interdependence makes conflict less likely because of its

efficiency over conquest in acquiring resources necessary for growth and prosperity. (2004, 547).[6]

And he finally arrives at the conclusion that

> [f]ree trade, and not just trade, promotes peace by removing an important foundation of domestic privilege—protective barriers to international commerce—that enhances the domestic power of societal groups likely to support war, reduces the capacity of free-trading interests to limit aggression in foreign policy, and simultaneously generates political support for the state often used to build its war machine. (ibid., 568–569)

Realists, on the other hand, disagree. Rather than mere commerce and interdependence itself, they tend to stress *relative* cost, that is, who will stand to gain more – or less – from trade-based interdependence. Dale C. Copeland, in the article 'Economic Interdependence and War', trying to find a mediating position between liberalism and realism, sums up his conclusions as follows:

> When expectations for trade are positive, leaders expect to realize the benefits of trade into the future and therefore have less reason for war now; trade will indeed 'constrain.' If, however, leaders are pessimistic about future trade, fearing to be cut off from vital goods or believing that current restrictions will not be relaxed, then the negative expected value of peace may make war the rational strategic choice. (Copeland, 1996, 39).

Katherine Barbieri, at almost the same time, put the realist position more starkly: 'Extreme interdependence, whether symmetrical or asymmetrical, has the greatest potential for increasing the likelihood of conflict' (Barbieri, 1996, 29), while Stanley Hoffmann, in his article on *Rousseau on War and Peace* (originally from 1965), predated the entire post-Cold War dispute by stressing that '[i]t is one of Rousseau's deepest insights, one that shatters a large part of the liberal vision of world affairs – that interdependence breeds not accommodation and harmony but suspicion and incompatibility' (Hoffmann, 1965/1987, 30).

If I were to choose, I would favour the (neo)realist position. It is backed by argumentative reason but most importantly by evidence: wars are still with

---

6 See also Lupu & Traag, 2012.

us; trade proliferates but has not been able to eliminate warring conflicts. *Inter*dependence does not annul *dependence*, but turns it into a question of relative gains in the anarchy of international relations, in spite of all manner of organisational 'moderating factors'. What's left of moral bias and optimism on this side is the still extant hope that *democratic* states would not go to war against each other. Or would they?

Debates and illusions concerning 'the democratic peace' (Gleditsch & Risse-Kappen, 1995; Henderson, 2002; Huntington, 1996, 198) conceal the common blind spot of both IR theories – what they both take for granted and simultaneously ignore: that the international system is made up of *states*, which both reflect their underlying economies *and* appear on the international stage as self-reliant power actors with their own independent interests and identities. In other words, their decisions concerning peace or war may or may not be motivated by economic considerations. Issues such as sheer power, sovereignty, independence, survival, territory, borders, vengeance or indeed national identity are often just as significant for people holding the reins of monopolistic power in a single state – whether they have been democratically elected or not. The question here is not one that pertains to the rationale of the state itself, understood as the conceptual outcome of domestic competition, but to the *existence of states in the plural*. This is the basic reason for war: that power monopolies eager to defend their most basic interests – in an interstate and imperialist competition for influence, resources, manpower, capital accumulation and prestige – have to interact, negotiate and come to terms with each other. This cannot but end in intermittent warring conflicts because states all have vested interests and 'red lines', which they cannot allow to be transgressed, if they are worth their salt as proper power monopolies with each their own 'amour-propre' (Rousseau).

The conflictual line between states hints at another pertinent observation: whereas *state in the abstract* is undoubtedly a product of the most basic contradictions of the capitalist system (between capital and labour, and between the competitive capitalist entrepreneurs themselves), *empirical states in the plural* epistemologically are not, but rather a consequence of historical factors extraneous to capitalism itself (uneven development, colonies and empires, the affective attachment of particular peoples to certain territories and power holders, etc.). Hence, power monopolies and capitalism historically have had to come to terms with each other.[7] On one hand, the corporate

---

[7] Charles Tilly has even argued that it is war making itself that historically led to states and their mutual rivalry (Tilly, 1985). It also provided the original impetus for the creation of state debt (Tilly, 1992, 74–75). Moreover, he realised that states and capital

world cannot be contained within the national framework, though it has generally managed to subordinate states to its growth rationale and stands to benefit enormously from them. It constantly pushes its own accumulative interests beyond national borders and turns states into foreign-policy actors with imperial designs. On the other hand, however, it also has to obey the bidding of its given political master and subordinate its interests to its decisions whenever the state finds itself in unmediated and non-negotiable conflict with other power monopolies. Thus, capital and nation states become linked, are interactive and mutually supportive, but are epistemically and teleologically different. Democratic rule naturally strengthens the link and makes the decisions of power holders legitimate, even when this means war.

4.

So, war is a confrontation of states, that is, monopolies of power, not of populations and not even of the corporate entities of capitalist competition. People (and companies as well) are subordinated to states and are forced to act as ideal or real representatives of states. They are the states' bases for calculation and manoeuvre. Hence, the (relative) truth that Rousseau articulated: 'War is then not a relationship between one man and another, but a relationship between one State and another, in which individuals are enemies only by accident, not as men, not even as citizens, but as soldiers; not as members of the fatherland, but as its defenders' (Rousseau, 1762/2017, Book 1, Chapter 4). However, 'men' (as soldiers) not only, willy-nilly, participate in and are indispensable for fighting the wars, they are, for the same reason, increasingly the victims of wars, whether traditional state wars or 'asymmetric' wars, where states fight armed 'terrorist' groups, mercenaries or private armies (Kaldor, 2012). Further, the victims of wars are far from only the conscripted or professional soldiers; increasingly, civilians have to bear the heavy brunt of armed conflicts, their numbers vastly exceeding that of the men in arms. They are injured, traumatised or killed in wars, whereas their states (and their political representatives) might well come out victorious or at least survive.

All systems, hence, for obvious reasons, want their peoples to back their wars, despite their sacrifices and often their unwillingness. In the words of an infamous fascist, who for once comes close to uttering a truth:

---

deserve differentiated treatment: 'Coercive means and capital merge where the same objects (e.g. workhouses) serve exploitation and domination. For the most part, however, they remain sufficiently distinct to allow us to analyze them separately' (Tilly, 1992, 19).

Naturally, the common people don't want war; neither in Russia nor in England nor in America, nor for that matter in Germany. That is understood. But, after all, it is the leaders of the country who determine the policy and it is always a simple matter to drag the people along, whether it is a democracy or a fascist dictatorship or a Parliament or a Communist dictatorship. [...] the people can always be brought to the bidding of the leaders. That is easy. All you have to do is tell them they are being attacked and denounce the pacifists for lack of patriotism and exposing the country to danger. It works the same way in any country.[8]

How 'simple' and 'easy' it is to make people back a war effort is doubtful. It might not be straightforward, but Göring's arrogant, slapdash judgement nevertheless hides an important truth: political leaders consciously use their power to manipulate the hearts and minds of citizens, while taking maximum advantage of their national loyalty and the gullibility citizens tend to show for the decisions of their political masters. In addition, his statement reflects the fact that, for a number of historical reasons, the Nazi project did resonate widely among, and managed to attract the support of ordinary Germans, who had also originally voted the Nazi Party into power and thus relinquished their own decision-making capacity. Henceforth, it is 'naturally' the political leaders 'who determine the policy'.

This is true even in democracies. When the political defenders of the Free World emphasise how difficult it is to safeguard the threatened peace – and this they regularly do[9] – they at the same time admit that they demand more of their citizens than they get when the same citizens 'merely' accept their daily plight and show loyalty in peacetime. Politicians address peaceful citizens' desire to be able to make do with their democratic rights and duties – only to refute it. For, according to the same political actors, it can only be fulfilled on the condition that the democratic order is defended and protected, even at the risk of the life and well-being of the same citizens. Freedom – as a 'higher value' – is apparently worth the price, in spite of the fact that people never get much out of it and in the case of war and attendant death definitely never will.

Nevertheless, wars cannot be initiated, and certainly not fought, without the backing of public opinion (Gallup, 1942), and in order to secure this backing, *morality* is crucial. It is necessary to mobilise citizens' moral bias for their

---

8 Herman Göring at the Nuremberg trials (Göring, 1946).
9 See e.g. Stoltenberg, 2021.

country in order for them to support wars. Other countries, the opponents and competitors, need to be framed as enemies and the representatives of pure evil (cf. Bush's 'axis of evil') and their populations as the dupes of scheming dictators intent on invading and conquering 'us'. The moral position is thus most easily mobilised and justified if you can present yourself as the victim or the defender, and at least as fighting for a righteous and legitimate cause (restoring the nation's pride, democratic liberties, 'our' cultural uniqueness, resisting the aggressor or what have you). Fascism or democratic rule – the role of *morality* is key. National identity, and the moralism it feeds on, here emerges as a means to maintain power and mobilise civilians.[10]

Nevertheless, democracies have a clear lead over fascist or other autocratic systems: their political 'class' has been duly elected by popular will and in this sense represents the national citizens, who are allowed the freedom of competition as private persons. They constitute the nation and its people, and whilst abstracting from their particular interests as private individuals, they have chosen their leaders within the framework of representative democracy. When push comes to shove, these leaders legitimately lead the nation into war, simultaneously abrogating the civil liberties of the citizens (see below). Hence, nations and not (just) states back the war, and (some) citizens are legally but also morally obliged to fight it, that is, to put their life on the line in support of the nation state.[11]

---

10 See for instance the statement of the Ukrainian defence minister on the subject of drafting male citizens living abroad: 'This is not a punishment for defending your country and serving the country. It is an honor' (Kyiv Post, 2023). On a similar note, the Danish prime minister, Mette Frederiksen, in an official announcement on 13 March 2024, legitimising the introduction of female conscription, insisted that 'defending your country is one of the most honourable things you can do' (https://www.dr.dk/nyheder/indland/regeringen-vil-indfoere-kvindelig-vaernepligt-paa-lige-fod-med-maend) (translation mine).

11 In passing, it must be mentioned that states also sometimes choose to rely on foreign fighters, mercenaries or people eager to show their willingness to risk their lives for x country in exchange for 'naturalisation', i.e. the alluring prospect of gaining citizenship. This can even become institutionalised, as is the case with the current US law providing for 'naturalization through military service', which has been in place since 2001 (see https://www.uscis.gov/military/naturalization-through-military-service). However, even applicants who 'have served honorably at any time in the U.S. armed forces for a period or periods totaling at least 1 year' must be able to '[d]emonstrate *good moral character* for at least five years before filing your N-400 through the day you naturalize' (italics mine). I am indebted to an anonymous reviewer for this point.

5.

War happens when all other means of power – economic, diplomatic, security-related – have been exhausted and have proved themselves incapable of producing the goal states pursue, that is, their national interests outside their own sphere of sovereignty. Clearly, making the transition from this kind of (conflict-ridden) peace into (all-out) war is not a decision made without seriously considering the costs of war and making sure that there is no other way forward. This is why war is generally considered an exception (a state of emergency) from the normal state of affairs,[12] and why there are probably many more examples of situations that might have led to war but didn't than there are of actual war occurrence (Blattman, 2022a and b). The costs are always huge and differentiated. Conducting wars involves gigantic financial expenses, both for the war effort itself and in terms of its deleterious effects on the civil economy; the loss of human lives (soldiers and civilians) is stupendous and has a severe impact on the financial, health-dependent and future situation of citizens and families; wars destroy both buildings (private, state or corporate) and the natural environment; and finally, though initially it cannot be fought without the support of the morale of the people and the soldiers, the war might well in the end have *de*moralising effects on both – with long-term consequences for – the state as well as the economy in the post-war period.[13]

For these reasons and many more, states will try to avoid the fact that conflicts escalate into open wars. Christopher Blattman has a point:

> The fact is that fighting – at all levels from irregular warfare to large-scale combat operations – is ruinous and so nations do their best to avoid open conflict. The costs of war also mean that when they do fight countries have powerful incentives not to escalate and expand those wars – to keep the fighting contained, especially when it could go nuclear. This is one of the most powerful insights from both history and game theory: war is a last resort, and the costlier that war, the harder both sides will work to avoid it. (Blattman, 2022a)

---

12 See Schmitt, 1922/1985; Schmitt, 1932/2007; Agamben, 2005.
13 'On average, a country that fights a war on its own territory will see a 12 per cent decline in its capital stocks five years after the end of that conflict relative to similar economies that do not experience a war (see Chart 1.17). Broadly speaking, historical experience suggests that it will take around 20 years for the capital stocks of advanced economies to return to levels consistent with the trends observed in comparator economies, while the capital stocks of lower-income economies tend to be permanently damaged by war' (European Bank for Reconstruction and Development, 2023).

War is indeed 'the last resort'. But Blattman overlooks two important, countervailing facts. One is that for states, economic considerations can and often do become subordinated to other 'issues' when conflict is pending and state (or alliance) interests (e.g. territorial, security-related, power-dependent, resource-oriented, systemic) are seriously threatened. In those cases, the 'honour' and 'values' of the state are foregrounded, the costs (economic or measured by human lives) dwindle into the background, and 'peace' has to be sacrificed to the higher good. The ongoing war in Ukraine is a case in point (see also below).

The second observation concerns Blattman's argument that '[t]he costs of war also mean that when they do fight countries have powerful incentives not to escalate and expand those wars'. This position overlooks the basic dynamic of wars, which, once started, cannot be masterminded, let alone controlled, by either side, precisely because the war situation involves a breakdown of (diplomatic) communications between the warring parties. Escalation by one side *has to be* met by escalation on the opposing side, until either one wins and the other is left as a loser by the wayside, or the situation remains deadlocked for an extended period, in which case the stalemate and war attrition may lead to a peace treaty or at least a truce. This dynamic, I argue, also applies to nuclear war: people who imagine that an exchange of nuclear weapons can be limited to 'tactical' weapons with 'manageable' destructive power delude themselves, whether they are professional strategists or ordinary citizens.

Concluding: war ultimately sets in when the *threat* to resort to the use of military means of power has proved to be ineffective. States prefer to avoid war if the threat of war is enough to make the enemy give in. But if not, they are willing to 'stake their all'.

Finally, it should not be overlooked that although wars are most often an economic 'loser' if regarded in the short-term perspective, they might nevertheless prove beneficial for victors in the long term. The United States, for instance, no doubt rose to the status of an economic (and military) superpower due to its role in WWII (Goodwin, 1992).

6.

As stated in Chapter 1, war factually nullifies all democratic practices (Crawford, 2021). Differences of opinion as well as tolerance are sneered at, elections are suspended and the parliamentary opposition rendered powerless, laws abrogated, the economy and its normal growth parameters totally subordinated to state objectives (see the next thesis), the material needs of citizens not even conditionally recognised, the sufferings of the 'citizen-soldier' glorified and open disagreement is regarded as treason.

He [the sovereign] decides whether there is an extreme emergency as well as what must be done to eliminate it. Although he stands outside the normally valid legal system, he nevertheless belongs to it, for it is he who must decide whether the constitution needs to be suspended in its entirety. (Schmitt, 1922/1985, 7)

In the ultimate 'emergency', everything is done in the name of 'exceptions', with the aim to secure the existence, honour and future progress of the state. War is, in other words, fascism in practice, as is military life and its command structures generally in 'times of peace', but as a sector separated from the rest of society.

The relatively copious literature on the similarities or differences between democracy and fascism hardly mentions this fact at all:[14] that in order to protect and maintain the democratic order, non-democratic methods that approximate those employed by the 'enemy', and which democracy is apparently diametrically opposed to, are enthusiastically embraced and employed. The reasons are many. The war situation is regarded as an exception from the normal state of affairs, and once 'we' have won, democracy will be reinstated. Democracy is slow and time-consuming, and in war, there is no time for that – decisions have to be made swiftly and decisively by the powers-that-be. Freedom of speech obviously cannot be permitted when the situation requires total agreement and a united front. And cool, level-headed analyses of the war are not just wrong-headed but downright treasonous, when we all need to back the state and relinquish our personal needs and opinions. In the end, the dearth of analytical and theoretical clarity in this regard comes down to the national bias of scholars and intellectuals (their partiality towards state, government and economy). Democratic methods in war are seen as an expendable luxury – something that speaks volumes about democracy itself and its purported goals.

However, the demand for absolute domestic unity in wartime also tells us another story about the dialectics of war and peace: war against 'the enemy' has to be backed by total domestic peace.[15] Carl Schmitt had an inkling of

---

14 See e.g. Dahl, 1989; Luebbert, 1991; Moore, 1968; Rader, 1943; Reiche & Blanke, 1972–73. A clear exception is Hecker, 1996.
15 Interestingly, this dialectic between outer war and inner peace also applied to the period between feudalism and early modernity, i.e. the fifteenth and sixteenth centuries, as Michael Walzer perceptively noticed in his *The Revolution of the Saints*: 'Expansion and aggrandizement became purposive and systematic, totally controlled by the same men who controlled the state. [...] Policy required discipline; no longer

this (1932/2007, 46), but was unable to carry the train of thought to its logical conclusion due to his fascist disposition, which connected 'total peace' with 'the normal state of affairs' rather than the 'exception'. He did realise, however, that war as the 'critical situation' mandated the state to 'decide upon the internal enemy', that is, the persons or groups that deserved to be declared 'traitors'. 'Total war' requires 'total peace', on pain of stigmatisation and death to those who do not follow suit.[16]

7.

In war, the peacetime relationship between state and economy is turned upside down. The economy is totally subsumed under the military purposes of the state, and the economic actors – partly the owners of property, partly the working people – not only have to accept (very different) limitations of their normal activities but must come to terms with their total subordination under the logic of war and the state's attempt, cost what it may, to come out of it victorious and thus defend its honour. No expenses of war and its conduct are, viewed from the perspective of the state, to be regarded as unnecessary – unless, that is, the war is lost. But in that case, the point of discussion is rather if *enough* resources were mobilized, if resources were deployed correctly, if the management of the war was at fault/inflexible/old-fashioned. Wars have their own economic logic, which is far removed from the 'normal' growth rationale of the competitive economies, which states enthusiastically support in peacetime.[17] In wars, states gluttonously devour all the money they can get for their own purposes, and the methods are, not surprisingly, taxation, borrowing and sometimes simple robbing and stealing.

---

was there room for the independent knight, the marauding baron with his feudal entourage, the local war; the state strove to suppress even the duel. And eventually the mercenary captains were brought into its service, morally transformed (up to a point) by the new aristocratic ethic of honor and public duty. *But the corollary of the King's Peace, thus established, was the king's war*' (italics mine) (Walzer, 1965, 273–274).

16 See e.g. Berlingske Tidende, 2023.
17 See this pertinent reflection by Professor Rosella Cappella Zielinski, author of *How States Pay for Wars* (Cornell UP, 2017): 'I always thought that when a state runs out of cash, the war stops. This is completely untrue. Besides the case of the Russians during the Russo-Japanese war, I have never seen a case of an interstate war ending because of money. It doesn't happen. Money isn't an inhibitor because there are so many opportunities to get it. I went into this subject thinking the state has a finite number of resources: it does not. The state can print money, go outside the country, collect diaspora remittances. There are simply so many places where the state can procure resources that money is not a barrier' (Rao, 2019).

8.

War short-circuits every vestige of truth. Information is distorted, misrepresented, prohibited and freely produced and circulated by the powers-that-be with a single purpose, that is, to win the violent showdown with the enemy. To this end, wars may become redefined as 'special operations', you may be imprisoned for using the *word* 'war', warfaring states deny terrorising civilian territory, fake news about enemy politicians, motives and failures get spread on social media, while the actions and results engendered on 'your own' side are described in heroic terms, and so on. All done to keep morale high among one's own population and armed forces, while – hopefully – undermining the morale (the 'fighting spirit') on the enemy side of the fence.

It is a common but trite saying that 'truth is the first victim of war' – as if factuality and truthfulness were the prime hallmarks of peacetime democracy. Alas, this is not so (Rosenfeld, 2018), no matter how intensely some scholars of 'fake news' would like this to be the case.[18] The difference between war and peace in this regard is not that the former produces nothing but lies and deception, and the latter honest-to-God truths, but that war extinguishes or suppresses the last remnants of factuality and truthful information that can be found in peacetime, for example, in news reporting and journalism, contributions of public intellectuals or scholarly publications. Democracy does not impose an absolute curfew on truthfulness but tries to adapt, accommodate or criticise it whenever necessary, keeping 'really sensitive' information well concealed from the public eye, whilst leaving all the remaining information and analyses in the safe hands of pluralist opinions and moralising tolerance.

9.

War is the unproductive destruction of life, property and nature. International law makes distinctions between 'wanton' and 'legitimate' ruination, war crimes and legally condoned actions of war,[19] but notwithstanding such legal niceties concerning Jus ad Bellum and Jus in Bello,[20] the result is invariably the same: people are maimed or killed, the natural environment polluted and material values destroyed. In the peace, which invariably follows, some of the material destruction will be rebuilt, values become recreated and social

---

18 However, on closer inspection, we find that they are often less concerned about truth than about the challenge of 'fake news' to people's trust in democracy and elected politicians. See e.g. Farkas & Schou, 2023.
19 Leebaw, 2014.
20 See ICRC, 2015.

institutions restored, but life has been annihilated for good and possibly the natural environment as well. The 'normal', democratic relationship of friction between states and citizens as well as interstate relations are restored on a new basis – favouring the victors – the economy is set moving again, financial institution start working as they used to, governments are elected or dictators grab power in military coups, while new reasons for war are being created.

10.

It follows from the preceding theses that it is not possible to get rid of war by rooting for peace but only by eliminating the reasons for war, which are invariably produced in peacetime. The first thesis stated that the relationship between peace and war is complementary. This is not to say that the difference is negligible; the relationship is not a gradualist one, but peace and war interchangeably define each other, meaning that peacetime as we know it is unthinkable without the permanent threat of war. For precisely that reason, all states and alliances of states do their utmost to keep a military capability and a military readiness which not only makes them able to withstand an attack but also to 'take the initiative', that is, to have the upper hand in an upcoming military confrontation.

Democratic states, contrary to usual assumptions regarding 'the democratic peace', exacerbate the problem for two reasons: first, they involve the people (as citizens), through elections and representation, in the run-up to conflict and war by appealing to their nationalism; and second, democratic states are always capitalist nation states, which conceal a built-in expansionist, imperialist drive. No matter how 'peacefully' they may act towards other states, they cannot, in the long run, avoid interstate conflicts, which may or may not be 'peacefully' settled, either because the weaker states choose to give in, or because the stronger ones manage to co-opt them into their (formal or informal) empires. This is the tendency that the EU represents. Here, morality again plays a central role: you can only become a member of the EU if you live up to specific values and respect the rule of law, minorities and human rights. Hence, the EU is often advanced as an argument to support the idea of 'permanent peace', where interstate conflict is settled by peaceful, diplomatic means:

> The European Union is one of many European institutions, but it is the most important one, and we see the EU (and its predecessors, the European Coal and Steel Community (ECSC), the European Economic Community (EEC) and the European Community (EC)) as a successful peace project. These bodies for European cooperation and integration

have indeed stopped the cycle of wars that tormented the European continent for centuries. (Lein, 2019)

On the other hand, this has not led to the member states relinquishing their military capabilities. Quite the opposite. Right now, they are all busy reinforcing them and giving maximum support to Ukraine in its fight against the Russian intervention, and they are more intent, than they have been for a long time, on spending 2 per cent of their GDP on defence and thus meeting the NATO requirements; some have even surpassed that standard – amongst them Poland. Yet, in spite of the EU's friendliness towards national minorities, the same cannot be said for its stance towards uninvited immigrants. Frontex does its best to keep them away from the European shores. In addition, EU member states are currently considering the establishment of asylum centres outside the EU: Denmark in Rwanda, Italy in Albania and so forth.[21] The peaceful continent is less peaceful when regarded through a microscope. War may have been abolished as a means to settle *internal* disputes, but this has just meant transposing the threat of violent conflict and war to a higher level. The reasons for war persist. They may even, at a later date, return to haunt the relationship with the transatlantic partner, where 'peace' also prevails, at least for now, because they can agree on having identical enemies.[22]

It is now time to briefly review the ongoing war between Russia and Ukraine, which epitomises many of the proposed theses.

The War in Ukraine: A Contemporary Case

Wars can assume different forms: direct or proxy wars, cold or warm, symmetrical or asymmetrical, offensive or defensive, conventional or nuclear, calculable or incalculable. The current war in Ukraine holds elements of all these. It is a proxy war with the largest and most potent (non-)combatant, NATO, standing on the sidelines, helping and cheering Ukraine and an imminent threat to Russia – at least from the Russian perspective. A seemingly asymmetrical, uneven war between David and Goliath, which for the same reason has become more even and confronts Russia with the same calculation that the United States must have been faced with in Vietnam, Syria, Afghanistan, and so on: Is it possible, wise or, for that matter, necessary to pass to the next threshold (e.g. chemical or tactical nuclear war); how would,

---

21 See Ruiz-Estramil, 2023.
22 Regarding the muddled EU situation regarding its place in the world and its changing relations with the United States, Russia and China, see Puglierin & Zerka, 2023.

in that case, NATO react; and has the final step towards a direct nuclear encounter then been taken? In the meantime, the Kremlin intimates that nuclear weapons are an option if NATO intervenes, and thus comes across as the cause of the escalation, something that also applies to the invasion of Ukraine itself: a tyrannical oligarchy, which for no obvious reason attacks a peaceful neighbour. This is the Western narrative. The Russian power monopoly may not be *that* crazy, however: in its own view of the world, it is *re*acting to a growing threat from NATO, feeling that Russia is in the process of being surrounded, pressurised and threatened in a number of ways. This then may be the old Western *containment* strategy from the Cold War in new clothes seen from the receiving end. Not only have many former Warsaw Pact countries now become members of NATO, but in several of them (Poland and Rumania, as well as Germany), anti-ballistic missile systems have been deployed, threatening to reduce the efficiency of Russia's nuclear potential. Hence, seen from Moscow, there is a difference between reasons for and occasions triggering war.[23]

NATO thus approaches a goal which has been all-important all along, that is, to make nuclear war not impossible, but calculable. In the '80s it succeeded in making the Soviet Union give in without a fight by arming the Eastern power to death ('totrüsten'). But Russia maintained and expanded its nuclear arsenal while simultaneously abandoning 'really existing socialism,' introducing private property and becoming a capitalist country run by a handful of oligarchs and their powerful state representatives, who were installed in order to protect the new order. The basis of the Russian economy is largely the production of raw materials (oil and gas, primarily) as well as agricultural produce. The GNP is comparable with Italy's, but Russia's ambitions far exceed this. Russia wants to be recognised as an international great power; the nuclear arsenal is the basis, and historical myths about (lost) Russian greatness and Western menaces fan the same flame and assume grotesque shapes when set against the contempt of the West and its much more expansive, economically motivated imperialism. It is no longer a question of a confrontation between two mutually exclusive economic-political systems, but one triggered by the refusal of the West to recognise Russia as a great,

---

23 What NATO is and why it exists should be no secret: it is an alliance unmistakably directed against Russia. Why else would a number of freedom-loving countries, which otherwise are competitors, join forces in a military alliance, if it were not to make a common threat go away? The naïve reaction that 'we' would all be safer if 'everyone' was a NATO member overlooks the simple fact that the *raison d'etre* of NATO ('collective security') *requires* an enemy. If there were no enemy, there would be no need for NATO, and the competition between the NATO members would be set free.

let alone a global power; the NATO members will not allow an economically speaking less significant state to possess a gigantic nuclear arsenal. Or, phrased differently, together with China, Russia stands in the way of the West's, especially the United States', claim to total and unlimited domination of the world market – their freedom, in other words – and must therefore be eliminated. Only then can peace take over (cf. thesis no 1).

So, Russia's war in Ukraine should be seen as a struggle for security and the survival of the Russian 'Self' – its interests, identity and honour – rather than the first step towards a recreation of the sphere of power and interests of the Soviet Union. That this struggle involves death, destruction and suffering on a gigantic scale is indisputable; in a belligerent conflict between states, there are no good guys but only room for calculating character masks. However, precisely for that reason, and for both sides in the conflict, the morality of 'just war' is more important than ever (Fisher, 2012). The political 'ultima ratio', which war represents, perforce has to come across as legitimate, justified, defensive, inevitable, the 'last resort' and supported by all the best arguments in the world; in other words, it must be rooted in moral considerations and a good political conscience. This obviously does not mean that either side seeks the support of the enemy based on such good intent; in war, all moral efforts are targeted towards the domestic population and 'one's own' soldiers, in order to brace them for the showdown with the enemy side with the right kind of mentality and fighting spirit; secondarily, the moralisation of war is aimed at winning over the sympathy of 'world opinion'. Whilst this naturally eliminates any kind of understanding or tolerance for enemy plans and actions and effectively annuls all freedom of speech in both Russia and Ukraine, the significance of the channels of mass communication and the contact between politics and the public sphere is augmented. Let us consider the morality question on either side more closely.

The Russian moral justification for releasing the war basically falls into three categories. One, Ukraine was on the point of becoming a NATO member, which would have meant that the Western alliance would have come dangerously close to surrounding the arch-enemy and would, so to speak, have been present on its very doorstep. In the Russian view, this was seen as an existential threat to its existence, and the Kremlin had been saying for years that this would be unacceptable. Second, the Russians accused Ukraine of attacking and discriminating against Russians and the Russian language in Donbas, and their invasion ('special military operation') was intended to put a stop to this and rescue their compatriots, while securing native Russian land for the Russian Federation. And third, the Ukrainian leadership allegedly consisted of fascists, and the Russian intervention was hence on a moral par with its resistance against the German Nazis during 'the Great Patriotic War'

(WWII).[24] It is clear that these arguments are mainly intended for domestic use, that is, for the Russian population and its morale. Particularly the third argument, however shaky it might sound, strikes a resonant chord with a core element in the Russian identity narrative, but also the other two are meant to justify the invasion as a defensive act rather than that of an aggressor attacking an innocent victim.

The Western moral argument, not surprisingly, runs somewhat differently. This is a consistent narrative about a monster empire (most often personified as 'Putin'), which illegitimately tries to take over a much weaker Ukraine, thus molesting its sovereignty and breaching all the rules in the international rulebook concerning 'just war'. It is a rogue dictatorship run amok, which desperately rustles up a bunch of fake reasons for its amoral actions, which are directed as much against the freedom-loving West as against Ukraine itself. Putin is a 'war criminal'. Russia is 'morally crippled'.[25] As Keir Giles, a Chatham House senior consulting fellow, expressed it in 2022, 'ensuring that Ukraine prevails is now the only moral choice'.[26] For this reason, it is naturally an obligation for the West and NATO to support Ukraine in every way possible: economically, politically, morally and militarily.

However, this simplistic narrative is not universally accepted, not even in the West. Listen, for instance, to Harvard professor Stephen Walt in a contribution to Foreign Policy (FP), 22 September 2023:

> Ever since the war began, those who favor giving Ukraine 'whatever it takes' for as long as it takes have sought to portray the war in the usual U.S. fashion: as a straightforward contest between good and evil. In their telling, Russia is solely to blame for the war, and Western policy had absolutely nothing to do with the resulting tragedy. They portray Ukraine as a struggling but plucky democracy that has been brutally attacked by a corrupt, imperialist dictatorship. They see the moral stakes as nearly infinite, because the outcome of the war will supposedly have a far-reaching impact on the future of democracy, the fate of Taiwan, the preservation of a rules-based order, etc. Not surprisingly, they are quick to condemn anyone who challenges this view as a naïve appeaser, a Russian lackey, or someone lacking any sense of moral judgment.

---

24 Further on 'just war' and the Russian argument, see Morkevicius, 2022
25 Politiken, 2023.
26 See Giles, 2022.

And he continues as follows:

> None of these claims should be accepted without qualification. There's no question Russia started the war and deserves to be condemned for it, but the claim that Western policy had nothing to do with it is risible, as NATO Secretary-General Jens Stoltenberg recently acknowledged.

The Stoltenberg reference is pertinent. It refers to an article in *Responsible Statecraft* three days prior to Walt's intervention (19 September 2023). In it, we find the following observation:

> It was curious to see NATO Secretary General Jens Stoltenberg earlier this month say explicitly that Russian president Vladimir Putin launched his criminal war as a reaction to the possibility of NATO expanding into Ukraine, and the alliance's refusal to swear it off – not once or twice, but three separate times.

The author of the article, Branko Marcetic, then astutely remarks that

> what Stoltenberg claims here – that Putin viewed Ukraine's NATO entry as so unacceptable he was willing to invade to stop it, and put forward a negotiating bid that might have prevented it, only for NATO to reject it – has been repeatedly made by those trying to explain the causes of the war and how it could be ended, only to be dismissed as propaganda.

Further down in the text, Marcetic substantiates his point in greater detail:

> You can find similar points in documents before the war. A 2020 U.S. Army War College paper states that 'future admissions to NATO for states in Russia's near abroad will likely be met with aggression.' A 2019 paper from the Pentagon-funded RAND Corporation – and sponsored by the Army Quadrennial Defense Review Office – states explicitly that the Kremlin's fear of a direct military attack by the United States is 'very real,' plus that 'providing more U.S. military equipment and advice [to Ukraine in the war on the Donbas] could lead Russia to increase its direct involvement in the conflict and the price it pays for it' including by 'mounting a new offensive and seizing more Ukrainian territory.' The 2017 National Security Strategy states outright that 'Russia

views the North Atlantic Treaty Organization (NATO) and European Union (EU) as threats'.

It's the central paradox of the current war discourse: What is widely acknowledged by Western policymakers and officials in the halls of power, who rely on an evidence-based understanding of the world to shape foreign policy, is unspeakable anywhere outside of them. [27]

What is interesting about what Walt termed a 'murky' argument is not just the direct tally with the first Russian war justification above, but also what the Western leaders make of their insight: not to give any kind of assurances to Russia concerning further NATO expansion (or the like), but rather to gloat over the 'unintended consequence' of the war, that is, that both Finland and Sweden have applied to become members. Stoltenberg: 'When President Putin invaded a European country to prevent more NATO, he's getting the exact opposite'. While Stephen Walt concludes his musings as follows, still sticking with the morality argument but with a realist addition: 'Ukraine's resolve has been extraordinary, and its desires should not be dismissed lightly, but this argument is not decisive. If a friend wants to do something you think is ill-advised or dangerous, you are under no moral obligation to aid their efforts no matter how strongly committed they may be. On the contrary, you'd be morally culpable if you helped them act as they wished and the result was disastrous'. In other words, if the power struggle indicates a different outcome than what you desire, morality will have to take second place or at least needs a revamp, in the best interest of 'the friend'.

Moral arguments are ubiquitously present but in different guises and serving different ends. For the Russians, they are needed to justify the invasion and create the proper backing and fighting spirit of the Russian people. For the Western alliance, they are needed to raise the right kind of outrage at the Russian atrocities and secure the support of both the ordinary citizen

---

27 For the whole article, see Marcetic, 2023. *The Guardian*'s Jonathan Steele has also offered a more plausible, non-moralistic analysis: '[f]rom outside the alliance [NATO], Putin has seen it expand continually. He says he does not seek a revived Soviet Union but a buffer zone that would be, as he put it in a long essay last year, "not anti-Russia". John Kennedy wanted a similar cordon sanitaire when Khrushchev tried to put nuclear missiles in Cuba in 1962', and '[c]onvinced that NATO will never reject Ukraine's membership, Putin has now taken his own steps to block it. By invading Donetsk and Luhansk, he has created a "frozen conflict", knowing the alliance cannot admit countries that don't control all their borders. Frozen conflicts already cripple Georgia and Moldova, which are also split by pro-Russian statelets. Now Ukraine joins the list' (Steele, 2022). The American political scientist John Mearsheimer has become (in)famous for a similar reading of the conflict. See e.g. Chotiner, 2022.

and 'world opinion'. By all and sundry, the war is portrayed as a moral fight between the forces of good and the forces of evil, and 'we' clearly have to support 'good' to the hilt. Enter moderating voices like that of Stephen Walt, who advocate a bit more prudence – because our Ukrainian friends might actually lose, and where would that leave us? Those friends themselves, of course, liberally exploit their moral high ground: they are a small, innocent, virtuous nation being brutally trampled on by the massive Russian war machine, while heroically defending themselves, their territory and their sovereignty.

However, not least in view of the above-noted alignment between Russia and NATO concerning the role of Ukraine in the confrontation between the two sides, it is not amiss to conclude that taking a stance either for or against either side based on moral considerations is wrong. Instead, it should be noted that while the Russians are engaged in frenetic bombing and the killing of people (soldiers and civilians alike) more or less indiscriminately on Ukrainian territory – with enormous losses, suffering and destruction as a consequence – the Western war alliance, NATO, has so far achieved its short-term goals without itself having to launch a single missile. By arming the Ukrainian military, it makes the Ukrainians do its dirty job for it; at the same time, it is able to monitor the performance of the Russian forces.

We often hear experts, journalists and ordinary citizens argue that what we are currently witnessing is, once again, a 'cold war', like the one that existed between NATO and the Soviet Union between the end of WWII and 1990, because Russia is regarded and treated as the main opponent – the arch-enemy – of the West, which regards it contemptuously, is determined to exclude it from the good international society and wants to make it recognise the absolute global dominance of the West/United States, both in market and political terms – one way or the other. The relationship is truly at a freezing point and Biden's 'slip of the tongue' in Warsaw (26 March 2022) – 'this man [Putin] cannot remain in power' –[28] expresses the American approach to the Russian regime in no uncertain terms: it is illegitimate and must be sent packing!

The analogy is faulty, however, because the confrontation is no longer a showdown between superpowers representing mutually exclusive political-economic *systems*. Both the West and Russia are capitalist – the latter since President Yeltsin donated to the private oligarchs a significant share of the public values in the 1990s: the so-called privatisation process.[29] Hence, the rivalry is now a different one, that is, (from the perspective of the West) to

---

28 Liptak & Vazquez, 2022.
29 See e.g. McFaul & Perlmutter, 1995.

recalibrate the link between the relative weakness of the Russian economy and Russian nuclear power, which is a thorn in the side of NATO – mainly the United States, global power number one, which is not willing to ignore this challenge. In other words, they want to force Russia to either voluntarily scrap significant parts of its nuclear capacity or make sure that the same is destroyed in a direct warlike encounter. Otherwise, 'we' won't be able to enjoy our peace and freedom, and Putin will continue to threaten us. You may well have to sacrifice your life in this encounter, but you should allegedly be grateful to have not just a nation, but an entire free world to defend, possibly mankind itself. However,

> [w]hen a state fights its political enemy in the name of humanity, it is not a war for the sake of humanity, but a war wherein a particular state seeks to usurp a universal concept against its military opponent. At the expense of its opponent, it tries to identify itself with humanity in the same way as one can misuse peace, justice, progress, and civilization in order to claim these as one's own and deny the same to the enemy. The concept of humanity is an especially useful ideological instrument of imperialist expansion, and in its ethical-humanitarian form it is a specific vehicle of economic imperialism. (Schmitt, 1932/2007, 54)

This is the enormous benefit of morality: it ensures that democratic states receive all the partial bias and undivided support they could wish for and that the states themselves appear as paragons of virtue rather than international actors with 'dirty hands'. This should not be taken to mean that morality and ethics are just a front concealing more nefarious goals. Rather, it displays the divided nature of the political scene in developed democracies: politicians, in all probability, do believe they are fighting for worthy causes and the best possible world, and they are willing to deploy whatever instruments are at hand to reach their goals, whether realistic or idealistic, belligerent or diplomatic, candid or clandestine. Where they are not willing to compromise is on the normative assessment of their activities. Here, there is no division, no dilemma. In their own view, they are on the right side of history, always fighting for 'the good' – no matter the sacrifices and no matter what 'real' considerations may have to stay hidden behind sealed bars. And sadly, they can rely on the support of their people and their national identity, due in no small way to the powerful influence of moral conviction and moral bias.

EPILOGUE

Go, go, go, said the bird: human kind
Cannot bear very much reality.

(T. S. Eliot)

For democratic politicians, morality is both instrumental and personally normative. It is an instrument to ensure that citizens properly internalise the behavioural 'code' matching politicians' social and political goals, such as 'personal responsibility, personal initiative, self-respect and respect for others and their property' (Thatcher, 1983). In domestic dealings with their power, they try themselves to observe such moral guidelines, if only to demonstrate that they belong to the same moral community as their subjects.

Nevertheless, they are not quite on a par with the rest of us. Sometimes they choose to engage in actions that, by ordinary standards, would be denounced as cruel, inhumane or downright evil, but this is not because they are bad persons; it follows from simply being engaged in politics. 'Politicians need to be judged by a political ethic where they can legitimately dirty their hands in the pursuit of worthwhile and noble goals' (de Wijze, 2019). In other words, we must understand that the moral standards of politics are different from those of civil society. This also applies to democratic politics. The ultimate proof of this is war, where politicians tend to embrace moral attitudes not just on behalf of their citizens and soldiers but on their own behalf as well. In such extreme cases, they abandon both legalistic constraints and material calculations and go the 'whole hog' for the sake of the nation's pride, identity and self-respect.

War is the touchstone of politicians' moral normativity, the point at which good must in the end conquer evil and where they are judged by higher standards than simply helping to protect private property and accelerate 'growth'. They must no doubt beware of the danger of committing 'war crimes', but in the heat of the moment, this matters less than victory and national honour.

Thus, political morality is a strange creature, always ready to provide political actors with the clean conscience they need when they set even the most horrific events in motion. The American political sociologist, Seymour Martin Lipset, in an introduction to the 1963 edition of *Political Man*, put the thought succinctly in characteristically downplayed fashion: 'The moralism that affects American foreign policy is not an unmixed blessing. It leads Americans to perceive other states as good or evil; and if a state is defined as an enemy and, therefore, the essence of evil, compromise with it is difficult, if not impossible' (Lipset, 1963, xxxi). Attack is construed as defence, 'our' deaths are heroic, the enemy is dehumanised, the conqueror a lover of peace. T. S. Eliot's feathered creature undoubtedly has a valid point: human kind cannot bear very much reality – but morality is a great help in cushioning the blow, even for hardened politicians.

REFERENCES

Agamben, Giorgio, 2005. *The State of Exception*. Chicago and London: University of Chicago Press.
Allison, Graham, 2017. *Destined for War: Can America and China escape Thucydides' trap?* Boston: Houghton Mifflin Harcourt.
Applebaum, Anne, 2019. Brexit has Devastated Britain's International Reputation — and Respect for its Democracy. *The Washington Post*, 12 March.
Antunes, Sandrina & Isabel Camisão, 2018. *Introducing Realism in International Relations Theory*. https://www.e-ir.info/2018/02/27/introducing-realism-in-international-relations-theory/. Accessed 26 May 2023.
Aron, Raymond, 1962/1973. *Peace and War: A Theory of International Relations*. Garden City: Anchor Press.
Astrup, Søren, 2023. Det er en rigtig god dag for Mette Frederiksen. *Politiken*, 24 May. https://politiken.dk/udland/art9363815/Bes%C3%B8g-i-Det-Hvide-Hus-er-milep%C3%A6l-for-Mette-Frederiksen. Accessed 31 May 2023. ['It's a Really Good Day for Mette Frederiksen']
Ay, Karl-Ludwig, 2004. The Meaning of Honour in Weber's Concept of the Nation. *Max Weber Studies*, Vol. 4, No. 2 (July), 221–233. London Metropolitan University: Department of Applied Social Sciences.
Barbieri, Katherine, 1996. Economic Interdependence: A Path to Peace or a Source of Interstate Conflict? *Journal of Peace Research*, Vol. 33, No. 1 (February), 29–49.
Basics, 2023. *Democracy vs Dictatorship with Facts*. https://www.basic-concept.com/c/democracy-vs-dictatorship-with-facts. Accessed 8 May 2023.
Berger, Peter, 1983. On the Obsolescence of the Concept of Honor, in Stanley Hauerwas & Alasdair MacIntyre, eds, *Revisions: Changing Perspectives in Moral Philosophy*. Notre Dame, IN: Notre Dame University Press, 172–181.
Berlingske Tidende, 2023. *Israelsk minister beskylder avis for sabotage af krig i Gaza*. https://www.berlingske.dk/internationalt/israelsk-minister-beskylder-avis-for-sabotage-af-krig-i-gaza, 24 November. Accessed 25 November 2023. ['Israeli Minister Accuses Newspaper of Sabotaging the War in Gaza'].
Blackman, Mathew, 2021. Does Law Exist to Provide Moral Order? *JStor Daily*, 15 December. https://daily.jstor.org/does-law-exist-to-provide-moral-order/. Accessed 3 March 2023.
Blattman, Christopher, 2022a. *The Five Reasons Wars Happen*. New York: The Modern War Institute at West Point. https://mwi.westpoint.edu/the-five-reasons-wars-happen/. Accessed 30 October 2023.

Blattman, Christopher, 2022b. *Why We Fight: The Roots of War and the Paths to Peace*. London: Penguin.
Bowman, James, 2006. *Honor. A History*. New York: Encounter Books.
Britannica, n.d. *Morality Play, Dramatic Genre*. https://www.britannica.com/art/morality-play-dramatic-genre. Accessed 1 December 2022.
Cambridge Dictionary, 2022. 'Tolerance' Entry. https://dictionary.cambridge.org/dictionary/english/tolerance. Accessed 23 November 2022.
Cannadine, David, 1990. *The Speeches of Winston Churchill*. London: Penguin.
Chotiner, Isaac, 2022. Why John Mearsheimer Blames the U.S. for the Crisis in Ukraine. *The New Yorker*, 1 March.
Clausewitz, Carl von, 1832/1976. *On War*, eds Michael Howard & Peter Paret. Princeton, NJ: Princeton University Press.
Copeland, Dale C., 1996. Economic Interdependence and War. *International Security*, Vol. 20, No. 4 (Spring), 5–41.
Crawford, Neta C., 2021. Democracy and the Preparation and Conduct of War. *Ethics & International Affairs*, Volume 35, No. 3 (Fall), 353–365.
Dahl, Robert A., 1989. *Democracy and Its Critics*. New Haven, CT: Yale University Press.
de Wijze, Stephen, 2019. Can Politicians Be Moral? *IAI News*, No. 73 (19 May).
Department of Defense, 2018. *Nuclear Posture Review*. Office of the Secretary of Defense. February. https://media.defense.gov/2018/Feb/02/2001872886/-1/-1/1/2018-NUCLEAR-POSTURE-REVIEW-FINAL-REPORT.PDF. Accessed 2 June 2023.
Devereaux, Bret, 2019. A Trip through Thucydides (Fear, Honor and Interest). *acoup.blog*. Accessed 15 May 2023.
Dönmez, Beyza Binnur, 2023. Hungary urges Sweden to Stop Spreading Lies on Country's Rule of Law. *Anadolu Ajansi (AA)*, 7 March. https://www.aa.com.tr/en/europe/hungary-urges-sweden-to-stop-spreading-lies-on-countrys-rule-of-law/2839484. Accessed 20 March 2023
Enlightio, 2022. *Why is Morality Important?* 13 December. https://enlightio.com/why-is-morality-important. Accessed 30 August 2023.
European Bank for Reconstruction and Development, 2023. Transition Report 2022–23: Business Unusual. *The Economics of War and Peace*. file:///C:/Users/sxz473/Downloads/transition-report-202223-the-economics-of-war-and-peace%20(3).pdf. Accessed 7 November 2023.
Farkas, Johan & Jannick Schou, 2023. *Post-truth, Fake News and Democracy: Mapping the Politics of Falsehood*. London: Routledge.
Fisher, David, 2012. *Morality and War. Can Wars be Just in the Twenty-first Century?* Oxford: Oxford University Press.
Formosa, Paul, 2008. 'All Politics Must Bend Its Knee before Right': Kant on the Relation of Morals to Politics. *Social Theory and Practice*, Vol. 34, No. 2, 157–181.
Gallup, George, 1942. How Important Is Public Opinion in Time of War? *Proceedings of the American Philosophical Society*, Vol. 85, No. 5 (September), 440–444.
Ghespière, Aude, 2024. The WEF in Davos - A Platform Boosting Swiss Prestige and Economy. *Leaders League*, 18 January. https://www.leadersleague.com/en/news/the-wef-in-davos-a-platform-boosting-swiss-prestige-and-economy. Accessed 5 February 2024.
Giles, Keir, 2022. *Ensuring Ukraine Prevails Is Now the Only Moral Choice*. The Royal Institute of International Affairs: Chatham House. https://www.chathamhouse.org/2022/04/ensuring-ukraine-prevails-now-only-moral-choice. Accessed 17 October 2023.

REFERENCES

Gilpin, Robert, 1981. *War and Change in World Politics*. Cambridge: Cambridge University Press.

Gleditsch, Nils Petter & Thomas Risse-Kappen, eds., 1995. Democracy and Peace. Special issue of *European Journal of International Relations*, Vol. 1, No. 4 (December).

Goodwin, Doris, 1992. The Way We Won: America's Economic Breakthrough during WWII. *The American Prospect. Ideas, Politics and Power*. https://prospect.org/health/way-won-america-s-economic-breakthrough-world-war-ii/. Accessed 18 October 2023.

Grau, Alexander, 2017. *Hypermoral. Die neue Lust an der Empörung*. München: Claudius.

Gurganus, Julia & Eugene Rumer, 2019. *Russia's Global Ambitions in Perspective*. Washington DC: Carnegie Endowment for International Peace, 20 January. https://carnegieendowment.org/2019/02/20/russia-s-global-ambitions-in-perspective-pub-78067. Accessed 19 April 2023.

Göring, Herman, 1946. *Interview with Gustave Gilbert in Göring's Jail Cell during the Nuremberg War Crimes Trial*, 18 April. https://www.mit.edu/people/fuller/peace/war_goering.html. Accessed 5 October 2023.

Hecker, Konrad, 1996. *Der Faschismus und seine demokratische Bewältigung*. München: Gegenstandpunkt Verlag.

Hedetoft, Ulf, 2020. *Paradoxes of Populism. Troubles of the West and Nationalism's Second Coming*. London and New York, NY: Anthem Press.

Henderson, Errol Anthony, 2002. *Democracy and War: The End of an Illusion?* Boulder, CO: Lynne Rienner.

Hitchcock, William I., 2018. *The Age of Eisenhower: America and the World in the 1950s*. New York, NY: Simon & Schuster.

Hoffmann, Stanley, Janus and Minerva, 1965/1987. Rousseau on War and Peace, in *Janus and Minerva. Essays in the Theory and Practice of International Politics*. Boulder, CO: Westview.

Holsti, Kalevi J., 1991. *Peace and War: Armed Conflicts and International Order 1648–1989*. Cambridge: Cambridge University Press.

Huntington, Samuel P., 1996. *The Clash of Civilizations and the Remaking of World Order*. New York, NY: Simon & Schuster.

ICAN (International Campaign to Abolish Nuclear Weapons), n.d. *What About Nuclear Deterrence*. https://www.icanw.org/what_about_nuclear_deterrence_theory?locale=en. Accessed 10 May 2023.

ICRC (International Committee of the Red Cross), 2015. *What Are jus ad Bellum and jus in Bello?* https://www.icrc.org/en/document/what-are-jus-ad-bellum-and-jus-bello-0%EF%BB%BF. Accessed 6 December 2023.

Jakobsen, Peter Viggo, Jens Ringsmose & Håkon Lunde Saxi, 2018. Prestige-seeking Small States: Danish and Norwegian Military Contributions to US-led Operations. *European Journal of International Security*, Vol. 3, No. 2, 256–277.

James, William, 1911. The Moral Equivalent of War. Lecture 11 in *Memories and Studies*. New York: Longman Green and Co, 267–296.

Johnson, Boris, 2016. Speech on the EU Referendum: Full Text. *Conservative Home*, 9 May.

Joshi, Shashank, 2008. *Honor in International Relations*. Cambridge, MA: Harvard University. Weatherhead Center for International Affairs, Working Paper no 08-0146 (December).

Kagan, Donald, 1997. Our Interests and Our Honor. *Commentary. Law, Government & Society*, April. https://www.commentary.org/articles/donald-kagan/our-interests-and-our-honor/. Accessed 5 March 2023.

Kaldor, Mary, 2012. *New and Old Wars. Organized Violence in a Global Era*. Stanford, CA: Stanford University Press.

Kant, Immanuel, 1795/1991. Perpetual Peace: A Philosophical Sketch, in Hans Siegbert Reiss, ed., *Political Writings* (pp. 93–125). Cambridge: Cambridge University Press.

Kant, Immanuel, 1797/1996. The Metaphysics of Morals, in Mary J Gregor ed., *Practical Philosophy* (pp. 353–604). Cambridge: Cambridge University Press.

Khong, Yuen Foong, 2019. Power as Prestige in World Politics. *International Affairs*, Vol. 95, No. 1 (January), 119–142. https://doi.org/10.1093/ia/iiy245. Accessed 25 March 2023.

Kyiv Post, 2023. *Defense Minister Umerov Considers Drafting Ukrainians Abroad*, 21 December. https://www.kyivpost.com/post/25783. Accessed 2 January 2024.

Kim, Youngho, 2004. Does Prestige Matter in International Politics? *Journal of International and Area Studies*, Vol. 11, No. 1, 39–55.

Kingseed, Cole C., 1995. *Eisenhower and the Suez Crisis of 1956*. Baton Rouge, LA: Louisiana State University Press.

Kovalik, Dan, 2021. *Cancel This Book. The Progressive Case Against Cancel Culture*. New York, NY: Hot Books.

LawTeacher, 2021. *Relationship between Morality and Law*. https://www.lawteacher.net/free-law-essays/medical-law/relationship-between-morality-and-the-law-medical-law-essay.php. Accessed 21 March 2023.

Leebaw, Bronwyn, 2014. Scorched Earth: Environmental War Crimes and International Justice. *Perspectives on Politics*, Vol. 12, No. 4, 770–788.

Lein, Jair van der, 2019. *The EU as Peace Project*. https://paxforpeace.nl/wp-content/uploads/import/import/pax-report-the-eu-as-a-peace-project.pdf. Accessed 1 December 2023.

Lipset, Seymour Martin, 1963. *Political Man. The Social Bases of Politics*. New York, NY: Doubleday, Anchor Books.

Liptak, Kevin & Maegan Vazquez, 2022. Biden Says Putin 'Cannot Remain in Power', *CNN Politics*, 26 March. https://edition.cnn.com/2022/03/26/politics/biden-warsaw-saturday/index.html. Accessed 15 September 2023.

Luebbert, Gregory M., 1991. *Liberalism, Fascism or Social Democracy: Social Classes and the Political Origins of Regimes in Interwar Europe*. Oxford: Oxford University Press.

Lupu, Yonatan & Vincent A. Traag, 2012. Trading Communities, the Networked Structure of International Relations, and the Kantian Peace. *Journal of Conflict Resolution*, Vol. 57, No. 6, 1011–1042.

Lytwyn, Matthew, 2018. *Nuclear Weapons and the Just War Tradition*. Center for Strategic and International Studies, May 16. https://nuclearnetwork.csis.org/nuclear-weapons-just-war-tradition/. Accessed 5 May 2023.

Mansoor, Peter R., 2015. *Why National Reputation Matters*. Stanford University: Hoover Institution.

Marcetic, Branko, 2023. When Officials say the Quite Part of Russia and NATO Out Loud. *Responsible Statecraft*, 19 September. https://responsiblestatecraft.org/russia-ukraine-nato-expansion/. Accessed 7 October 2023.

Markey, Daniel, 1999. Prestige and the Origins of War: Returning to Realism's Roots. *Security Studies*, Vol. 8, No. 4, 126–172.

Martin, Susan B., 2013. The Continuing Value of Nuclear Weapons: A Structural Realist Analysis. *Contemporary Security Policy*, Vol. 34, No. 1, 174–194.

REFERENCES

Marx, Karl, 1867/1977. *Das Kapital*, Erster Buch. Marx-Engels Werke (MEW), Vol. 23. Berlin: Dietz Verlag.

McDonald, Patrick J., 2004. Peace through Trade or Free Trade? *Journal of Conflict Resolution*, Vol. 48, No. 4, 547–572.

McFaul, Michael & Tova Perlmutter, eds., 1995. *Privatization, Conversion, and Enterprise Reform in Russia*. Boulder, CO: Westview Press.

Miliband, Ralph, 1973. *The State in Capitalist Society*. London: Quartet Books.

Millett, Peter, 2014. The Worst Form of Government. Foreign, Commonwealth and Development Office. https://blogs.fcdo.gov.uk/petermillett/2014/03/05/the-worst-form-of-government/. Accessed 18 May 2023.

Moore, Barrington, 1968. *Social Origins of Dictatorship and Democracy*. Boston: Beacon.

Morgenthau, Hans J., 1949. *Politics among Nations*. New York, NY: Alfred A. Knopf.

Morgenthau, Hans J., 1979. *Human Rights and Foreign Policy*. New York, NY: Council on Religion and Foreign Affairs.

Morkevicius, Valerie, 2022. How do Russia's Reasons for War Stack Up? *The Conversation*, 5 March. https://theconversation.com/how-do-russias-reasons-for-war-stack-up-an-expert-on-just-war-explains-178135. Accessed 23 November 2023.

Mosely, Alexander, n.d. Just War Theory. *Internet Encyclopedia of Philosophy*. https://iep.utm.edu/justwar/. Accessed 20 May 2023.

NATO, 1995. *NATO Handbook: Partnership and Cooperation*. Brussels: NATO Office of Information and Press.

New World Encyclopedia, 2023. *Scramble for Africa*. https://www.newworldencyclopedia.org/entry/Scramble_for_Africa. Accessed 12 June 2023.

O'Neill, Barry, 1999. *Honor, Symbols, and War*. Ann Arbor, MI: University of Michigan Press.

———, 2002. *Nuclear Weapons and the Pursuit of Prestige*. Draft, Department of Political Science, University of California Los Angeles, May. http://www.sscnet.ucla.edu/polisci/faculty/boneill/prestap5.pdf. Accessed 6 May 2023.

———, 2003. Mediating National Honour: Lessons from the Era of Dueling. *Journal of Institutional and Theoretical Economics*, Vol. 159, No. 1, 229–247.

Pakenham, Thomas, 1992. *The Scramble for Africa*. London: Abacus.

Peristiany, John George & Julian Pitt-Rivers, eds., 2005. *Honour and Grace in Anthropology*. Cambridge: Cambridge University Press.

Politiken, 2023. *Rusland er moralsk forkrøblet*, 17 November. ['Russia is Morally Crippled'].

Puglierin, Jana & Pawel Zerka, 2023. *Keeping America Close, Russia Down, and China far Away: How Europeans Navigate a Competitive World*. Policy Brief, European Council on Foreign Relations, 7 June. https://ecfr.eu/publication/keeping-america-close-russia-down-and-china-far-away-how-europeans-navigate-a-competitive-world/. Accessed 6 August 2023.

Rader, Melvin, 1943. The Conflict of Fascist and Democratic Ideals. *The Antioch Review*, Vol. 3, No. 2 (Summer), 246–261.

Rao, Kapu, 2019. How Do States Pay for Wars? *Phenomenal World*, 3 May. [Interview with Rosella Cappella Zielinski.].

Rawat, Sandeep, 2022. *Tolerance*. https://www.quora.com/What-are-some-examples-of-tolerance-from-your-daily-life. Accessed 12 December 2022.

Reiche, Reimut & Bernhard Blanke, 1972–73. Capitalism, fascism and democracy. *International Journal of Politics*, Vol. 2, No. 4 (Winter), 19–46.

Rosenfeld, Sophia, 2018. *Democracy and Truth: A Short History*. Philadelphia: University of Pennsylvania Press.

Rousseau, Jean-Jacques, 1762/2017. *The Social Contract. Chapter IV: Slavery*, ed. Jonathan Bennett. https://www.earlymoderntexts.com/assets/pdfs/rousseau1762.pdf. Accessed 4 June 2023.

Ruiz-Estramil, Ivana Belén, 2023. Asylum? Maybe, But Outside the EU. The Externalization of the Responsibility to Protect, 14 March. https://blogs.law.ox.ac.uk/border-criminologies-blog/blog-post/2023/03/asylum-maybe-outside-eu-externalization-responsibility. Accessed 25 August 2023.

Runciman, David, 2018. *How Democracy Ends*. London: Profile Books.

Schmitt, Carl, 1922/1985. *Political Theology. Four Chapters on the Concept of Sovereignty*. Translation and Introduction by George Schwab. Chicago and London: University of Chicago Press.

Schmitt, Carl, 1932/2007. *The Concept of the Political*. Translation and Introduction by George Schwab. Chicago and London: University of Chicago Press.

Stanford Encyclopedia of Philosophy, 2022. *Moral Theory*. https://plato.stanford.edu/entries/moral-theory/. Accessed 22 March 2023.

Stanford Encyclopedia of Philosophy, 2023. *The Problem of Dirty Hands*. https://plato.stanford.edu/entries/dirty-hands/. Accessed 1 December 2023.

Steele, Jonathan, 2022. Understanding Putin's Narrative about Ukraine is the Master Key to this Crisis. *The Guardian*, 23 February.

Stoltenberg, Jens, 2021. *NATO 2030 - Safeguarding Peace in an Unpredictable World*. Keynote Speech by NATO Secretary General Jens Stoltenberg at the Sciences PO Youth & Leaders Summit, 18 January. https://www.nato.int/cps/en/natohq/opinions_180709.htm. Accessed 10 September 2023.

Strachan, Owen, 2019. *"I am Here to Save the Honor of France": Charles de Gaulle and the American Future* (providencemag.com). Washington DC: Institute on Religion and Democracy. Accessed 25 March 2023.

Streeck, Wolfgang, 2017. *How Will Capitalism End?* London: Verso.

Thatcher, Margaret, 1983. *Speech to Scottish Conservative Conference*, 13 May. https://www.margaretthatcher.org/document/105314. Accessed 18 January 2024.

Thornton, Bruce, 2017. Prestige as a Tool of Foreign Policy. *Defining Ideas*, 12 June. Stanford University, Hoover Institution. https://www.hoover.org/research/prestige-tool-foreign-policy. Accessed 15 May 2023.

Thucydides, 1910. *The Peloponnesian War*. London: J. M. Dent.

———, 1998. *The Landmark Thucydides: A Comprehensive Guide to the Peloponnesian War*, ed. Robert B. Strassler, 1st edn. New York, NY: Simon & Schuster.

Tilly, Charles, 1985. War Making and State Making as Organized Crime, in Peter Evans, Dietrich Rueschemeyer & Theda Skocpol, *Bringing the State Back In*. Cambridge: Cambridge University Press, 169–191.

Tilly, Charles, 1992. *Coercion, Capital, and European States, AD 990–1992*. Oxford: WILEY Blackwell.

Trump, Donald, 2021. *Remarks by President Trump in Farewell Address to the Nation*. Washington DC: The White House, 19 January. https://trumpwhitehouse.archives.gov/briefings-statements/remarks-president-trump-farewell-address-nation/. Accessed 2 May 2023.

United Nations, n.d. *International Day for Tolerance: 16 November*. https://www.un.org/en/academic-impact/international-day-tolerance-16-november. Accessed 30 June 2023.

REFERENCES

United States Conference of Catholic Bishops, 2023. *Morality*. https://www.usccb.org/beliefs-and-teachings/what-we-believe/morality. Accessed 12 December 2023.

Walsh, Jim, 1997. Surprise Down Under: The Secret History of Australia's Nuclear Ambitions. *The Non-Proliferation Review*, Fall, 1–20.

Walt, Stephen, 2023. The Morality of Ukraine's War is Very Murky. *Foreign Policy*, 22 September.

Walzer, Michael, 1965. *The Revolution of the Saints. A Study in the Origins of Radical Politics*. Cambridge, MA: Harvard University Press.

Walzer, Michael, 1977. *Just and Unjust Wars*. New York, NY: Basic Books.

Weber, Max, 1921/2009. Politics as Vocation, in *From Max Weber: Essays in Sociology*, eds, Hans Gerth & Charles Wright Mills, prefaced by Bryan S. Turner. London: Routledge, 77–129.

Welsh, Alexander, 2008. *What is Honor? A Question of Moral Imperatives*. New Haven and London: Yale University Press.

Wikipedia, 2023. *Just War Theory*. https://en.wikipedia.org/wiki/Just_war_theory. Accessed 31 August 2023.

Wood, Steve, 2014. Nations, National Identity and Prestige. *National Identities*, Vol. 16, No. 2, 99–115.

Yogeeswaran, Kumar, Levi Adelman & Maykel Verkuyten, 2021. The U.S. Needs Tolerance More than Unity. Tolerance Allows us to Live in Harmony Despite Deep-seated Differences. *Scientific American*, 2 March.

Ziady, Hanna, 2023. Too Big for Switzerland? Credit Suisse Rescue Creates Bank Twice the Size of the Economy. *CNN Business*, 24 March. https://edition.cnn.com/2023/03/23/investing/credit-suisse-ubs-impact-switzerland/index.html. Accessed 6 May 2023.

Zielinski, Rosella Cappella, 2017. *How States Pay for Wars*. Ithaca, NY: Cornell UP.

www.ingramcontent.com/pod-product-compliance
Lightning Source LLC
Jackson TN
JSHW021946080625
85732JS00009B/24